Uniforms & Equipment of the Austro-Hungarian Army in World War I

Uniforms & Equipment of the Austro-Hungarian Army in World War I

Spencer A. Coil

Schiffer Military History
Atglen, PA

ACKNOWLEDGMENTS

First, and foremost, I would like to acknowledge and dedicate this work to all those who served in the Great War, especially to those who appear in these photographs and above all to my family, who supported and stood by every step of the way in the creation of this work, especially my mother!

I would like to thank the following individuals who directly or indirectly assisted in the creation of this work:

Vladimir, Irina, and Natalie Pomeranzera-Halikin (experts and enthusiasts)
Alexei Grichine (expert and specialist)
The Ezzo Family particularly, Diplom Ingeneur Blahad Ezzo (enthusiasts)
Frau Dr. Grafin Irene Montjoye and her son Herr Mag. Graf Douglas Montjoye
(authors, journalists, enthusiasts, historians)
Dan Eibeck (expert, specialist, enthusiast, historian)
George Steinwenker (expert, specialist, enthusiast)
Peter Coeln, of the Leica Shop and Westlicht Camera and Photograghy Museum
located in the Westbahnstrasse 40, A-1060 Vienna, Austria
President Dr. Wil Goodheer
Vice-President Dr. L. Boyer
President Dr. David Harpool
Professor Del Schwinke
My Students

A special thanks to the internationally acclaimed and recognized military medals and decorations experts, specialists and enthusiasts Herr und Frau Mag. Hartmut und Christine Rochowanski who have maintained an impecable reputation for over thirty years and Franz Zabernig. I am also very grateful to my special friend Karl Machherndl whose pieces from his and his father's collection, who served in the First World War, appear in this work.

Book design by Robert Biondi.

Library of Congress Catalog Number: 2003106376

Printed in China.
ISBN: 0-7643-1869-1

We are interested in hearing from authors with book ideas on related topics.

Published by Schiffer Publishing Ltd.
4880 Lower Valley Road
Atglen, PA 19310
Phone: (610) 593-1777
FAX: (610) 593-2002
E-mail: Info@schifferbooks.com.
Visit our web site at: www.schifferbooks.com
Please write for a free catalog.
This book may be purchased from the publisher.
Please include $3.95 postage.
Try your bookstore first.

In Europe, Schiffer books are distributed by:
Bushwood Books
6 Marksbury Avenue
Kew Gardens
Surrey TW9 4JF
England
Phone: 44 (0) 20 8392-8585
FAX: 44 (0) 20 8392-9876
E-mail: Bushwd@aol.com.
Free postage in the UK. Europe: air mail at cost.
Try your bookstore first.

Contents

	Introduction	6
Chapter One	Machine Gunners	9
Chapter Two	Pioneers	26
Chapter Three	Life on the front	33
Chapter Four	Air Corps	70
Chapter Five	Anti-Aircraft	102
Chapter Six	Telegraph	108
Chapter Seven	The Blumenteufel (Edelweiss collar insignia)	121
Chapter Eight	Dragoons	150
Chapter Nine	Hussars	162
Chapter Ten	Uhlans	164
Chapter Eleven	Kraftfahrer und Kraftfahrzeug (Motorists and vehicles)	170
Chapter Twelve	Medical	183
Chapter Thirteen	Berndorfers and Austrian Stahlhelms	193
Chapter Fourteen	Bosnians	201
Chapter Fifteen	Eisenbahn (Railroad)	212
Chapter Sixteen	General Infantry (All ranks)	218
Chapter Seventeen	Hundetraingespann (Dog transport teams)	246
Chapter Eighteen	Kaiser Jaeger	251
Chapter Nineteen	Ersatz/ Unusal/ Private Purchase	258
Chapter Twenty	Artillery and Artillerists	282
Chapter Twenty-one	The Kaisers (Franz Joseph and Karl)	317
	Vignettes	321
	Color	322
	Glossary	342
	Appendix	344
	Further Reading	352

Introduction

Belonging to the Central Powers, the Austro-Hungarian Monarchy was a dual monarchy consisting of the empire of Austria and the kingdom of Hungary. The monarch, up until July 1916, was Kaiser Franz Joseph I. Franz Joseph I was emperor (*Kaiser*) of Austria and king (*Kiraly*) of Hungary. Upon his death in 1916, his grand nephew, Erzherzog Karl, took his place as both emperor and king.

Both of these Kaisers exerted a tremendous influence on the style of the royal and imperial soldier (the *k.u.k.)*. Either their initials, (FJI, IFJ or K) on cockades or their distinctive profiles on decorations appeared in the daily life of every soldier serving his Kaiser on the battlefield.

The Kaisers influenced even the cut and style of the tunic. An example of this can be seen in the mid to late war tunic, the Charles' tunic (*der Karl's Bluse*). The classic tunic worn by a *k.u.k.* soldier during the reign of Franz Joseph I was single breasted with either interior or exterior breast and side pockets with a two-scallop flap and with either a stand or fall collar. Cuffs had to follow army regulations (*Vorschriften*), but this was not rigidly enforced.

In contrast, *der Karl's Bluse* maintained the same over all cut but varied in design by the use of only exterior pockets with pleats and exterior buttons. Again, the collars were either stand or fall.

Despite the Kaisers' influence and army regulations, the individual soldier sought to enhance whenever possible his clothing or outfit (*Bekleidung or Montur*) beyond that of what was issued to him at the depot. He did this by privately purchasing materials and services from royally and imperially commissioned court suppliers (*k.u.k. Hof Lieferants*) or private craftsmen.

For example, most depot-issue tunics were made of a high quality grade of either *Feldgrau* or *Hechtgrau* wool which was stamped at the depot. However, if the soldier could afford another material which he found more practical or even more fashionable, such as gabardine, corduroy, or another grade of wool, he would have it made privately, adhering to the overall cut set forth in the army regulation manual. The practice of private purchase meant other colors, such as stone gray (*Steingrau*), could be used as well.

A *k.u.k.* soldier's field cap (*Feldmütze*) was also subject to the same influences and regulations. As with a tunic, a soldier was issued a field cap made of the same types of wool and with depot stamps. The design of the field cap was practical because it offered some protection to the ears and throat during harsh weather conditions. Nevertheless, privately purchased field caps were very common, particularly those made of pressed and crushable felt. This was a private purchase even an enlisted man could afford and often bought. Often soldiers would wear a coarse, wool, rolled stocking cap with a non-functional cockade and buttons. Normally, these items provided a function on field caps, such as the buttons held the side flaps in place and the cockade served as a vent.

The most important accessory for the *feldmuetze* was the cap badge (*Kappeabzeichen)*. These badges varied in size, shape, material, craftsmanship and motif and could be purchased privately by every soldier. Sizes ranged from one-half inch to three inches, and shapes conformed to the motif. Most *Kappeabzeichen* were made of tin, iron, enamel, or bronze. Precious metals, such as gold and silver and other metals, such as brass and aluminum (which, at the time, were considered precious), were also used. Patriotic badges and pins worn by soldiers and civilians alike, were made of polished stone, ceramic or wood. *Kappeabzeichen* were mostly die-stamped with the name, and often the address, of the manufacturer on the reverse side. *Kappeabzeichen* were also cast, which was not as popular amongst the soldiers because the cast badges were heavier than the lightweight and durable stamped badges. Patriotic badges and pins were often carved or cast and then enameled.

Kappeabzeichen motifs, which were expressed and explained not only in German, the *lingua franca*, but also in other languages of the multinational dynastic empire, ranged from the heroic, humorous, dramatic, religious, mythological, medieval, and macabre. Heroic motifs depicted a *k.u.k.* soldier standing alone against the overwhelming enemy forces or bravely standing watch. Other heroic motifs showed entire regiments charging fiercely into battle with bayonets fixed and banners waving or holding the line. Humorous motifs, particularly those concerning the southern front, showed the *k.u.k.* soldier simply disciplining the delinquent enemy by spanking, smacking or giving him the boot to the backside.

Dramatic motifs depicted dying or wounded soldiers being consoled or treated. Such motifs were common for medical unit badges and pins. Religious motifs included angels, saints, crucifixes, the Virgin Mary, Christ crowned with thorns and Islam's moon and star. The cavalry cap badges often depicted a dragoon, hussar or an *ulan* mounted and praying before a crucifix with his helmet off. (The cap badge of the Epidemic Spital Trient depicted the face of Christ crowned with thorns and the *Landstrum Infantrie Regiment Nr. 25* depicted the Virgin Mary with child watching over the battlefield.) Artillery Units depicted St. Barbara, the patron saint of artillerists. Bosnian, Turkish, and certain patriotic cap badges featured Islam's moon and star. There were even cap badges made for religious holidays such as Christmas, Easter and Yom Kippur. Mythological motifs included depictions of Mercury, as seen on the badge from the *Feldtransportleitung Nr. 9*, Icarus, who was very popular with aviators (flieger*)*, and Apollo, as seen on the *Honved Infantrie Regiment Nr. 302* badge. Medieval motifs, particularly those depicting knights, are seen on some badges, such as on the *Heeres Gruppe Erherzog Eugen,* showing a triumphant knight, or the 21st Korps showing a knight with an edelweiss on his shield and his sword sweeping over the Alps protecting and ridding them of invaders. Macabre motifs, such as skulls and crossbones (*totenkopf*), or crossed grenades, or skeletons (*skelett*) appeared later in the war with the arrival of the storm troopers (*Sturmtruppen*). The *Sturmtruppen* evolved from mechanized warfare, and their ranks were made up of soldiers who experienced its horror from 1914 onward. It is, therefore, understandable that they would have such macabre motifs on their cap badges. Examples of these motifs can be seen on such badges as the fourth *jaeger* division (a skull with crossed grenades) or the Hungarian 51st division or *M. kir. 51 honved hadosztaly roham zaszloalj* (an oval wreath, framed *Sturmtruppen* loaded with stick grenades accompanied and guided by a skeleton).

When not made to depict the afore-mentioned motifs, cap badges were enameled or stamped metal numbers, letters, oak leaves, pine bows, helmets, and the Kaisers' and Generals' profiles or busts. The most simple and popular amongst soldiers were the Tyrolean eagle or edelweiss cap badges. Both appeared in many different shapes, sizes and materials and became the symbols of the *k.u.k.* soldier to the enemy. The edelweiss earned the soldiers the name "flower devils" (*blumenteufel)* from their enemies, and the Tyrolean eagle,(*Standschützen Baon Meran)* cap badge symbolized tenacious defense of the home (*heimat*). These symbols were even popular to wear on the home front as patriotic badges and pins.

Silk or cotton ribbons (*Kappeabzeichen*), with or without patriotic sayings, were worn on the *Feldmütze*. The ribbons were in the official colors of the monarchy, black and the Emperor's gold (a deep yellow). One popular patriotic saying which appeared on many ribbons was "*Heil ins Feld*" or "Safe and sound on the battlefield."

It is important to note that *Kappeabzeichen,* as well as medals and other decorations, were worn by soldiers on the battlefield, not just for studio photos or while on leave, or on parade. For these occasions, the soldier would have purchased an extra medal or had the medal duplicated. When having one privately made, the soldier could choose a more precious material and could often even have a box made to place it in to keep it in good condition for these occasions. This practice even applied to other equipment, such as helmets. For example, if an officer could afford it, he would have his helmet reproduced in a lighter weight material, such as aluminum or cork. M16 *Stahlhelms*, for example, can be found in aluminum. Aluminum was considered a precious metal and was difficult to obtain because of the allied blockade. However, the resourceful soldiers could obtain the aluminum by collecting older model canteens or from captured enemy equipment.

As much as the *Feldmütze* and its various interpretations represented the *k.u.k.* armed forces, the fez, as worn by the Bosnians, represented an elite and admired branch of the army as well as the multiethnic composition of the Hapsburg Empire. Fezzes were either red or field gray and varied in size and shape. It was just as popular for soldiers to wear *kappenabzeichen* on a fez as it was on a *Feldmütze.*

Fezzes were worn in civilian life and were often taken as souvenirs by other soldiers. These fezzes differed from military fezzes in two ways. The first difference was in construction. The fez used in the field had to be much more durable than its civilian counterpart. The second difference was military fezzes had two loops stitched parallel to one another, which held a regimental badge in place. Privately purchased as well as depot-stamped fezzes were worn in the military.

Perhaps the most popular cloth headdress was the "walking out" or "dress" cap *(Ausgangskäppi)* in black (*schwarz).* Although officially reserved for dress, it was often worn in the field. One branch of the military which regularly made the *ausgangs kaeppi* a part of their *montur* was the Air Corps (*Fliegerkorps*).

Since the *Fliegerkorps* was relatively new and made up largely of volunteers, regulations were not rigidly enforced. Therefore, each *Flieger* or aviator sought to enhance his appearance by more decadent dress than his comrades in the other branches of the military. The A*usgangskäppi* is one of many examples of the aviators' robust and adventuresome style. It is understandable this style would appeal to those in a new branch of the military, and any innovation was welcomed.

Aviators reflected many of the styles of the motorists (*Kraftfahrer*) who were also relatively new to the battlefield and the cavalry, a noble yet archaic branch of the military, who were slowly becoming obsolete. The *Kraftfahrer*, like the aviators, were exposed to wind and weather as they sat in their open cockpits. (Windshields for the *Kraftfahrer* proved to be more of a hazard than a benefit while driving on or near the front because the concussion from an explosion would shatter it.) This exposure prompted the need for clothing which would keep out wind, cold and rain. Thus, leather became the obvious choice for caps, tunics, jackets and pants. Aviators, having even more exposure to the elements, wore leather flight masks which often had goggles sewn in the mask. It was also popular, as well as practical, to line *Montur* with various furs. Most leather gear was privately purchased because of cost, shortage of leather goods and need for a custom fit.

Good visibility and eye protection was essential for both. Various designs of goggles (*Brille*) were worn. Design could mean an increase or decrease in peripheral vision. One design which increased peripheral vision was goggles with folding glass lenses. These glass lenses were capsule shaped and jointed in the middle which enabled them to conform to the face. Eye protection was difficult to ensure since lenses were made of either glass or celluloid.

As much as new innovations in *Montur* design was of importance to the aviator, the early colorful pomp of the cavalry remained popular as most of the aviators came from the ranks of the cavalry.

Because of changes in battlefield tactics and technologies, the Austrian cavalry, as with cavalries of other nations, saw its final glorious days in the First World War. Trench warfare and the emergence of the machinegun made a cavalryman's duty very hazardous. Nonetheless, the cavalry was useful for rapid deployment and eventually had its own mounted machinegun units.

The use of horses and cavalry remained, however, in an altered capacity. Horses were used for transport, beasts of burden, and, in desperate times, as a source of food. Eventually, many of the cavalrymen blended into other ranks.

The cavalry wore their colorful uniforms in the field officially until 1915, and afterwards, only for dress. The headdress of the cavalry also changed after 1915. The M. 1850 *Dragoon* helmet, M.1871 *Hussar shako*, and M. 1899 *Ulan tschapka* with their shiny metal fittings made the wearer an easy target and therefore needed to be modified. The modifications included painting the helmets *hecht* or *feldgrau* or covering the helmets in fabric. Although aviators had no use for heavy and cumbersome helmets, *shakos* or *tschapkas*, occasionally they would don the red forage cap (*Schiffchen)* of the cavalry. Frequently, aviators would wear the cavalry uniforms, with the only alterations being balloon collar insignia sewn to the collar or perhaps two parallel loops sewn to the right side of the tunic to hold a flight badge.

Another evolving branch of the *k.u.k.* forces from which the air corps drew volunteers was the artillery. *K.u.k.* forces used both old and new models of artillery pieces. Throughout the war, artillerists modified pieces according to need and function. Standard factory features and regulation and instruction manuals (*Vorschriften*) proved not to always meet the demands of the front. Therefore, as modifications were made on the front, the instruction manuals were handwritten as there was no time or any means to produce printed manuals explaining the functions and modifications.

Initially, artillery was divided into three categories: field, mountain and fortress artillery. Field (*Feld*) and mountain artillery (*Gebirgsartillerie*) was the most versatile and could be easily transported and deployed. Fortress artillery (*Festungsartillerie*) included heavy mortars, such as the 30.5 cm *Mörser*, which were used to destroy heavily fortified positions, such as those at Przemysl. Technical support groups were also assigned to artillery units which included telephone operators and observation crews and equipment. Artillery units were often attached to Air Corps units as anti-aircraft to protect the aerodromes. Aviators would often wear brown tunics with red cuffs worn by artillerists early in the war, and then later only for dress or parade, altering them the same as the cavalry tunics.

The end of the First World War and the passing of the monarchy did not immediately alter the *Bekleidung* or *Montur* of the Austrian soldier in the First Republic (*Erste Republik*), also referred to as the inter war period (*Zwischen Kriegs Zeit*). This was largely due to the impending material shortage and the disorganization and destruction of most industry. Nevertheless, a new look was evolving for the soldiers of the First Republic which reflected the nostalgia of the Monarchy while incorporating styles and innovations of neighboring countries, first and foremost being their former and soon-to-be future ally, Germany.

The first to alter the style of their *Bekleidung* or *Montur* was the standing army of the First Republic (*Erste Republik Bundesheer* or *Erstes Bundesheer*). This was first evidenced in the headdress, as they switched from the *k.u.k.* style *Feldmütze* to the circular visor cap which resembled a mixture of the Czech visor cap of the 1920's and 30's, the German NCOs or officers' caps in World War I and the *Freikorps* of the 20's and 30's. The Austrians' *Teller Kappe,* which literally translates "plate cap," bore the crest of a province and a cockade with the colors of the First Republic, red and white. The *Bundesheer* still wore a *feldmuetze,* however, the shape was different in that it was more round and cylindrical than that worn by the *k.u.k.* armed forces. The tunic collars also changed by adopting a German cut and with cloth strips (*Litzen*) stitched to the collar indicating rank. Equipment marking and stamping also changed from the *M.D. (Montur Depot)* or *B.A. (Bekleidungs Amt)* to *HBA (Heeres Bekleidungs Amt)* plus the date.

The style and often even the original *k.u.k.* uniforms, with slight alterations, remained basically the same in the ranks of paramilitary groups such as the Home Guard (*Heimwehr*). The Home Guard was largely made up of proud veterans from the First World War. One alteration that was distinctly characteristic of a First World War tunic used by a member of the Home Guard was a cap or collar insignia from a *k.u.k.* machinegun or telegraph unit sewn to the left sleeve with a green diamond-shaped cloth backing. Although most members of the Home Guard were supporters of the former monarchy, most First World War insignias used were "de-monarchized" in that the crown was removed. For example, the crowns on the double-headed eagle (*Doppel Adler)*, a classic symbol of the monarchy, were replaced with halos (*Heiligenschein*).

The Home Guard and other paramilitary groups, and even their rivals, the Socialists (*Sozialisten*), kept the culture of wearing and collecting the cap badges alive. Cap badge motifs of this period still echo those from the First World War, especially the eagles, edelweiss and *Stahlhelms*. Other motifs commemorated their marches, meetings and events.

Chapter One

Machine Gunners

3 NCOs in the Balkans in 1915 with a *Schwarzlose* machinegun. The soldier on the left, whose rank is concealed because of a collar cover, is holding a M95 *Stutzen* (short rifle). The lid on the ammo box appears to slide shut, whereby most ammo box lids lifted up.

Machinegun unit on the southern front in 1916. Two different mounts for the *Schwarzlose* can been seen as well as larger ammo boxes, both painted and unpainted, with lift-up lids.

A machinegun unit practicing on a range in 1916.

A 1917 photo of machine-gunners showing off their bayonets. The three soldiers in the middle have the ersatz or "*not*" bayonets. The "*not*" bayonet was a mid to late war invention. Normally, the blade did not have a blood groove and the handle lacked wooden grips.

A hand held/mobile machine squad (H.G.M *Handmaschinengewehr Zug)* from the Jaeger Regiment No. 4 in 1916. The *Schwarzlose* is shown with a bipod.

A machinegun unit in 1916. All wear the wood frame ammunition backpacks, each of which would carry four 50-round boxes. 50-round boxes were preferred because the small size was easy to carry, therefore increasing a machinegunner's mobility especially in mountainous terrain.

A machinegunner in 1917 who has been awarded the Franz Joseph I bravery medal in bronze and the *Kaiser Karl Truppen Kreuz.*

Machinegunners on a road in the Alps in 1917. The wood frame backpacks are used for transporting ammunition. Dogs often assisted in transporting weapons and equipment.

A "*MGK*" or *Maschinengewehr Kompani*e in 1915. The two soldiers in the center belong to a Jäger Regiment and the soldier to their left has been awarded the 1st and 2nd class Kaiser Karl bravery medal in silver. The machinegun badges, worn above the right breast pocket, were abandoned later in the war.

A machinegunner in 1917 who has been awarded the Kaiser Karl bravery medal in silver 2nd class, the Franz Joseph bravery medal in bronze and the *Kaiser Karl Truppen Kreuz*.

Two machinegunners in 1915. The NCO on the left wears a private purchase felt hat, and the officer wears the popular *Ausgangskäppi in schwarz* (walking-out or dress kepi in black).

Early war machinegun unit.

Machinegunner wearing *feldgrau* (field gray) in 1917. The cockade with the letter "K" stands for Kaiser Karl.

A *Leutnant* (lieutenant) who has been awarded the Kaiser Karl bravery medal in silver 2nd class, bronze bravery medal and the Kaiser Karl Truppen Kreuz. 1917.

Pre to early war machinegun unit firing atop a bluff in the Balkans.

Machinegunners on the southern front in 1916. This mount for the Schwarzlose helped increase the maneuverability and allowed the gunner to change his direction of fire more easily.

Machinegunners in 1916. The two soldiers on either side carry M95 *Stutzen* (short rifle). Although the small or assault ammo box held only 50-rounds, it was easier to carry and was not as cumbersome as a large ammo box.

Machinegunners on the eastern front in 1915.

Machinegunners on the eastern front in 1915.

Machinegun unit on the Isonzo front with captured Italian Fiat-Revelli Model 1914 machinegun.

Machinegunners in the Dolomites with captured Italian Fiat-Revelli Model 1914 machine. Soldier on the left holds on M95 *Stutzen* (short rifle).

Machinegunners on the southern front in 1917. The lighter colored uniforms are summer weight. The soldier on the ground in the center is holding a trench periscope.

Machinegunners in the Balkans 1915. Note the unusual red cross patch which has been stitched to the tunic's sleeve. Normally, the medics wore an arm band which slid on and off.

Pre to early war machinegunners. Later in the war, machinegunners rarely wore their badges as seen over the right breast pocket of these soldiers.

Machinegunners on the southern front in 1917.

Machinegunners on the eastern front anxiously awaiting an attack in 1915

This corporal wears an issue tunic with private purchase gabardine pants.

Fähnrich or cadet. 1914.

Machinegunner with the rank of Korporal from the Landwehr Infantrie Regiment No. 1 on the eastern front on August 15th 1915.

A machinegun unit in Albania. Many soldiers in this unit have won bravery medals, such as the silver bravery medal 1st and 2nd class and the bronze bravery medal. 1918.

Machinegunners in the Dolomites using a captured Maxim-Vickers Model 1911. Soldier on the right holding the binoculars has been awarded the bronze bravery medal. 1917.

Chapter Two

Pioneers

First Lieutenant (*Oberleutnant*) in the Pioneers wearing patriotic rings and a compass. 1916

Pioneers examining a destroyed railroad bridge on the eastern front in 1915.

Pioneers building trenches on the eastern front in 1915.

Pioneer on a destroyed railroad bridge on the eastern front in 1915.

Pioneers on the eastern front with standard issue shovels. Shovels were normally stamped with unit numbers (e.g., I.R. 4 - Infantry Regiment No. 4). This photo was taken in 1915.

A studio photo of a pioneer taken in 1916. He wears a Franz Joseph I cap badge on his issue hat. His uniform is issue as well.

A Pioneer of enlisted rank wearing *Ledergamaschen* (leather gaiters). He carries a Pioneer saber and a M95 stutzen. 1916

Pioneers constructing a railway bridge on the eastern front in 1915.

Pioneer with the rank of *Zugführer* on the Danube in 1915.

Zugführer or platoon leader in 1917. The *abzeichen* or badges above his right breast pocket were very popular amongst the soldiers, and many purchased them privately. Normally, these badges were considered *Kappeabzeichen* or cap badges and were worn on their *feldmuetze* or field caps.

Pre to early war studio photo of a pioneer with the rank of Gefreiter. He wears a Sapper's badge (*Sappeurauszeichnung*) as well as a Worker's badge (*Arbeiterauszeichnung*).

k.u.k. Gesteinbohr Bataillon (k.u.k. Rock Drilling Battalion) in the Dolomites. 1916.

k.u.k. Gesteinbohr Bataillon (k.u.k. Rock Drilling Battalion) in the Dolomites. 1916.

Chapter Three

Life on the Front and In the Trenches

December 22, 1915 on the southern front. The soldier holding the skis has been awarded the Kaiser Karl bravery medal 2nd class in silver. The soldier in the center holds an M95 *Gewehr*.

Soldiers of the 4th Battalion on the southern front in 1917.

The ruins of a church on the eastern front. 1915.

Soldier on the shores of the Black Sea near Odessa in July 1916.

Standing outside a *Wachzimmer* or guard room, these soldiers display three distinct variations of ammo pouches for the M95. The soldier on the front left wears the classic and most often seen M95 ammo pouch. The soldier in the middle wears a late war ammo pouch (made of zinc or lead or a *Kriegsmetall* wartime composite metal. The soldier in back far right wears an earlier ammo pouch. All carry the M95 *Gewehr.*

Soldiers at rest on a hillside in the Balkans. Soldier on the far right is a medic attached to a machinegun unit. He sits atop a carrying harness which was made to fit over the back of a mule.

Soldier in the trenches on the eastern front reads the sign which indicates the doorway marks the left flank of this platoon's sector of the line. 1915.

Soldiers of the *6./87 Feld Kompagnie* at rest in the trenches after a trench raid. 1915.

Soldier standing by a firing hole on the eastern front in 1915

Sentries and an officer inspecting barbed wire fortifications on the southern front. 1917

A sunny day in the trenches on the southern front. 1916.

Trenches on the eastern front in 1915.

Soldiers of the *Landsturm Infantrie Regiment No*. 2. 1916

Soldiers of *Jäger Regiment No. 3*. equipped with gas masks in their canisters.

Granatenwerfer position on the eastern front in 1916. Box on the right is for ammunition.

Soldiers of the *k.u.k. Infantrie Regiment* Albert I Koenig *der* Belgier Nr. 27 in an observation post on the eastern front. August 1915.

Soldiers at rest after a long march. 1916

A machinegunner pausing to observe a shrine of the Virgin Mary. Southern front, 1917.

Winter on the eastern front in 1915. Soldier on the right has been awarded the Military Jubilee Cross.

A sniper taking aim from a well fortified position on the Isonzo front. 1917

Soldiers cleaning their rifles on the Isonzo frontline. 1917.

Officers in the trenches on the southern front in 1916. Officer on the right has been awarded the Kaiser Karl bravery medal 1st class in silver. The hole on the left is known as a "*Füch's Loch*" or fox's hole. This could shelter one soldier during a bombardment.

Soldier of the 13th Corps during a cease fire on the southern front in 1917.

Soldier at rest on the eastern front in 1916. The major in the center has been awarded the German Iron Cross.

Soldiers of the *k.u.k. Infantrie Regiment Freiherr von Bolfras No. 84* trying to make their section of the line look more like home. 1916.

Soldier on their way to the southern front pause to eat some watermelon. 1916.

Field kitchen and bakery on the southern front. 1917.

Mail call on the southern front. 1917.

Soldiers on leave. Southern front, May 20, 1918.

Trenches on the eastern front. 1915

The bathhouse for officers and enlisted men of the *Infantrie Regiment No. 75*

Soldiers of "*Korps Hoffmann*" awaiting an attack. 1916.

Soldiers of the 13th Corps having lunch. 1915.

Soldiers camped in a forest near the southern front. 1917.

Soldier takes aim from his firing hole inside a bunker on the southern front. 1917.

Two officers on the southern front in 1917. Officer on the left has been awarded the military service cross, military service medal in silver and bronze, and the *Kaiser Karl Truppen Kreuz*. Both are wearing private purchase field caps with a gold stitched "K" with crown instead of a cockade.

Soldiers ready for a gas attack on the southern front. 1917.

Soldiers on the western front. April 1918.

Soldiers enjoying life at the front. Soldier in the middle wears an edelweiss made of *Kriegsmetall*. It looks as though the five are sitting next to a *Minenwerfer*, however the long pipes are for an oven.

A supply depot (*Montur Depot/ Bekleidungs Amt*) in Brunn in 1916.

Two bronze bravery medal winners wearing private purchase pressed felt forage caps (*Schiffchen*) in the Alps. 1917.

Soldiers enjoying a drink on the eastern front in 1915.

Soldiers awaiting a meal on the southern front. 1916.

Not only does this soldier display a sense of humor, but also, an unusual style of pants with leather reinforcement. On the floor lies a private purchase crushed felt hat and an ammo pouch for the Rast and Gasser revolver. Eastern front. 1915.

Hungry mice attacking what is left of a soldier's meal next to his pre to early war aluminum canteen. This canteen (*Feldflasche*) fit inside a specially made pouch in a soldier's bread bag. 1918.

Soldiers inspecting their mounts in the Balkans. 1915.

A soldier on the southern front in 1917 posed with his "loyal friend." He carries a field gray enamel canteen on a string. Normally, the canteen had a cloth cover with wood peg fasteners and an adjustable cloth-carrying strap.

Soldiers camped in the Balkans. 1915.

Austrians with a German *Kamerad* on the southern front in October 1917. *Gefreiter* on the left has won a silver bravery medal second class. *Gefreiter* on the right wears a *Karl's Bluse*. Both wear *Pantalons* or pants with reinforced leather knees.

Soldiers on the southern front. January 28, 1917.

Soldiers outside a dugout on the eastern front. 1915.

Officers planning an attack inside a bunker on the southern front in 1917. Officer on the right has been awarded the silver bravery medal 2nd class and the bronze bravery medal.

Soldiers posed in front of a field kitchen (*Feldküche*) on the southern front. 1917.

Southern front. February 10, 1918.

Southern front. 1917. The four soldiers on the outside wear issued uniforms and equipment. Also seen are two different types of belt buckles. First, the doubled headed Hapsburg eagle which was normally made of brass, zinc, or painted iron. Second, a single prong buckle. Double prong was also used although not seen here.

Major of the *Landsturm Infantrie Regiment Ji_in No. 11* emerging from a dugout. 1916.

Soldiers examining the rubble after an artillery bombardment. Eastern Front. 1915.

Soldiers at rest and enjoying a smoke on the eastern front in 1915.

Soldiers in the trenches on the southern front. 1917.

Officer in the trenches on the eastern front. 1916.

Soldiers enjoying a smoke and a game of cards on the eastern front. 1916.

Soldiers at rest on the southern front. 1917. The soldier in the front row on the right has been awarded the silver bravery medals 1st and 2nd class, the bronze bravery medal, and the Kaiser's Jubilee Cross. The soldier standing on the right wears the silver bravery medal 1st class and a Red Cross medal. The other soldier wears the silver bravery medal 2nd class and the Kaiser's Jubilee Cross.

Soldiers on the eastern front in 1916. Hanging from the center tent pole is an Austrian bread bag.

Soldiers in the trenches on the southern front. 1916.

Soldiers enjoying a drink with the ladies. Soldiers on the far left and in the middle holding a bottle belong to a Motor Corps (*Kraftfahrer*) unit as their collar insignias and breast badges indicate. Soldier on the far right is wearing a summer weight tunic and field cap.

Soldier resting atop a bell on the eastern front. 1915.

Soldiers at rest on the southern front. 1916

Soldiers camped in a forest on the eastern front. 1915.

Chapter Four

Air Corps

Everything a pilot had at his disposal: *Schwarzlose* MG M 7/12; *Madsen* MG M15 with magazines in a leather case; 7.63mm **Mauser** with extended wooden stock; flare pistol with flares; *Fliegerpfeile* (literal translation, "aviator arrows" known by the allies as fleschettes or iron darts) in wooden carrying case; 18kg and 40kg *Woellersdorf* **bombs**, 20 kg *Carbonit*, two 1kg *Woellersdorf Brandpfeile* (literal translation, "burning or flaming arrow" otherwise known as an incendiary device), and four *Leuchtsatz* (flash bombs) with parachutes.

Aviator (*Flieger*) with the rank of *Leutnant* on southern front near the Piave in 1917. He wears a private purchase gabardine *Karl's Bluse* and *Schiffchen*. The artillery buttons indicate that he was attached to an artillery unit before volunteering for the Air Corps (*Fliegerkorps*). Balloon insignia, as seen on his collar and cap, were worn by all in the *Fliegerkorps*.

Aviator with the rank of *Oberleutnant*. He wears the general airman's badge (*Allgemeines Luftfahrerabzeichen*) on the right breast pocket of his *Karl's Bluse*. He has also been awarded a bravery medal.

An aviator with the rank of *Oberleutnant* southern front near the Piave in 1917.

Aviator with the rank of *Oberleutnant* on the southern front near the Piave in 1917. He wears a summer weight *Karl's Bluse* and his artillerist's *Ausgangskäppi*. The black dress kepi was very popular with the air corps.

An aviator with the rank of *Leutnant* on the southern front near the Piave in 1917. Crossed swords on the bravery ribbon bars were awarded for combat.

A *Leutnant* from the 1st Kaiser Jäger Regiment in a gabardine *Karl's Bluse*. July 13, 1918.

A *Gefreiter* in a field gray (*feldgrau*) issue tunic. 1916.

A *Leutnant* in 1916. Since the aviators were volunteers, there were fewer regulations for them to follow, particularly with their dress.

Aviator in *feldgrau*. 1916.

Aviators in a forest on the southern front in 1917. Aviator in the back is removing film from his camera after a reconnaissance patrol. Aviator in front row right wears a white summer weight tunic and forage cap (*Schiffchen*).

Aviators reading newspapers and mail on southern front in 1918.

Aviators doing custom tailoring on a sewing machine in the field in 1917. Aviator in front of the sewing machine is holding a field telephone.

Aviator with the rank of *Feldwebel* on the southern front in 1917. He has been awarded the silver service cross.

Austrian and German aviators enjoying drinks after a good meal. Southern front. 1917.

Austrian and German aviators enjoying drinks and a good war story. Aviator in the middle holds what is left of a propeller. Southern front. 1917.

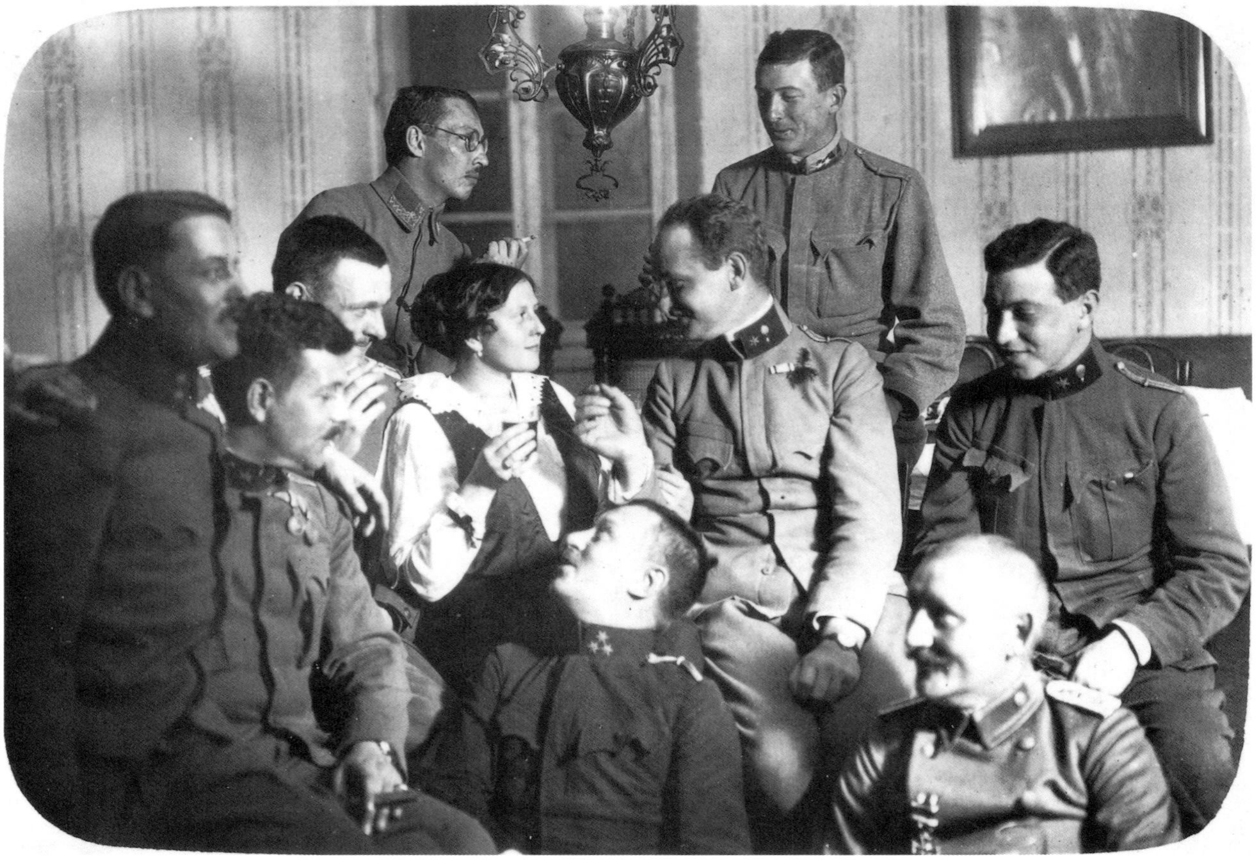

Austrian and German aviators enjoying a drink in the parlor with a lady. Southern front. 1917.

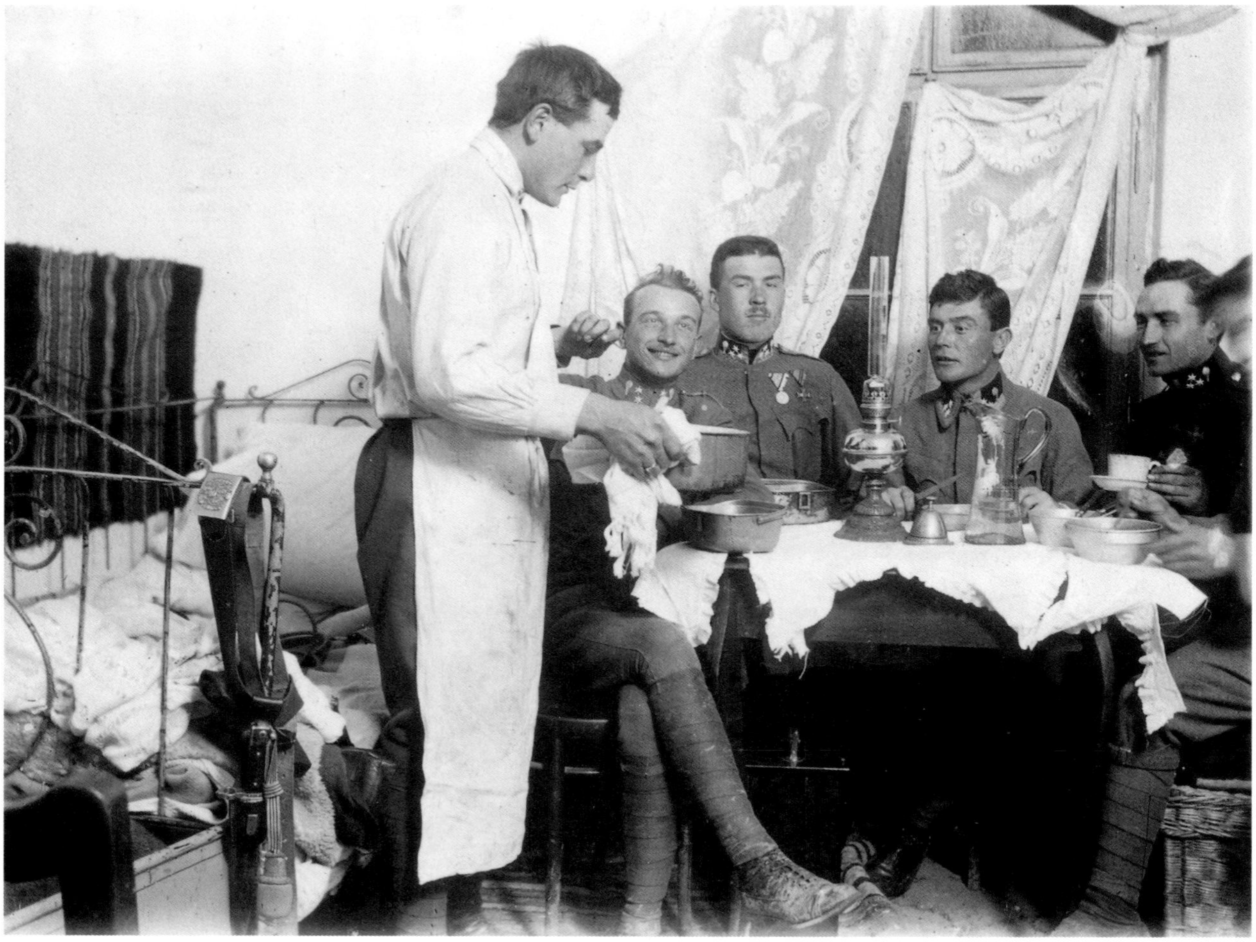

Aviators anxiously awaiting their dinner. Southern front. 1918.

Aviators enjoying drink and a game of cards while one calls on the field telephone to invite some more *Kameraden* to join in the fun.

Aviators arriving to enjoy drink and conversation Southern front. 1917.

Aviators enjoying a lot of drink and conversation. Southern front. 1917.

Aviators enjoying a whole lot of drink and conversation. Southern front. 1917.

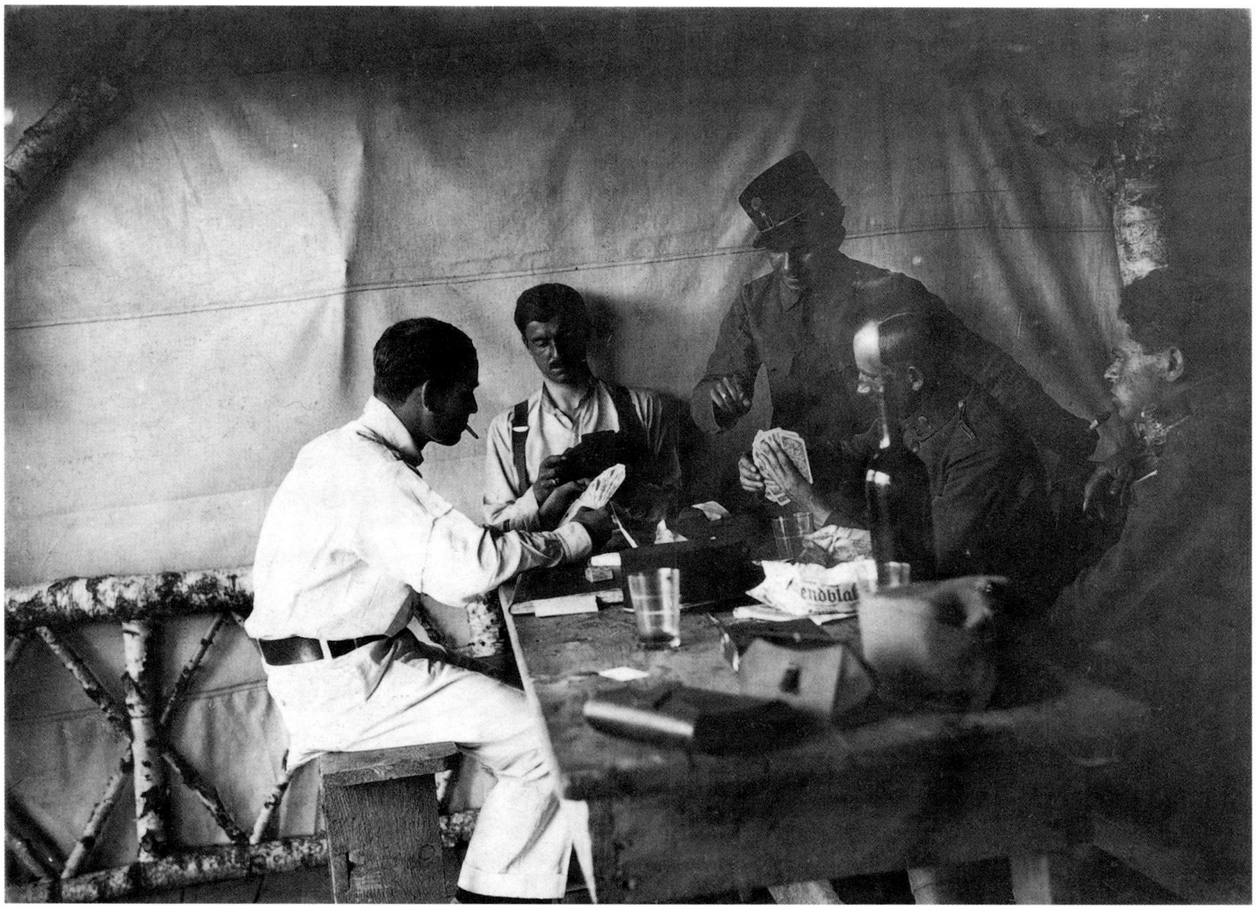

Aviators playing cards on the southern front in 1917.

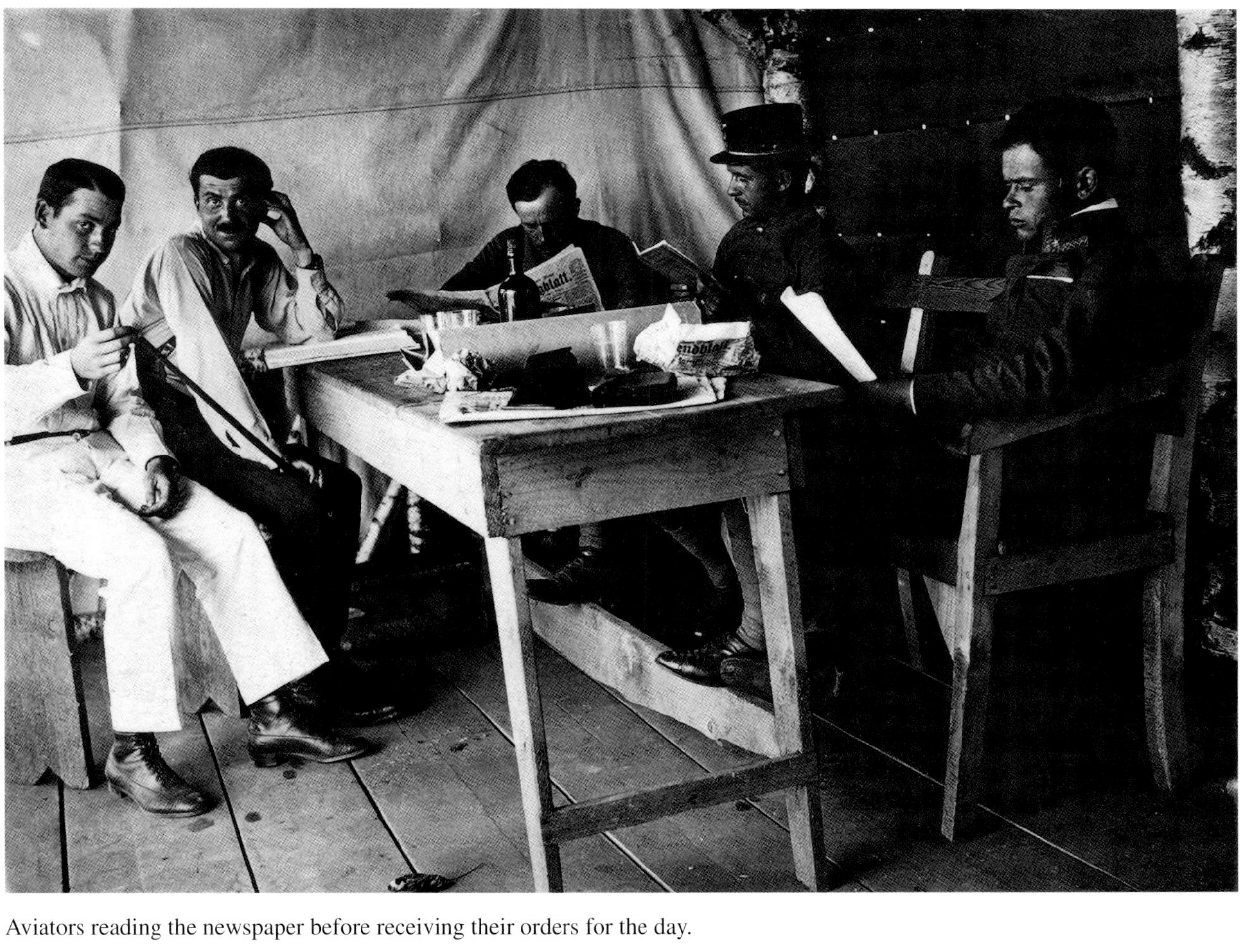

Aviators reading the newspaper before receiving their orders for the day.

Aviators pause for a drink. Southern front.1917.

Aviator with the rank of *Oberst* examining fuselage rib. Southern front. 1917.

Aviators resting after a flight.

Although not the best at flying, the dog was as much apart of this squadron, or *Staffel*, as anyone else. The forage cap "*Schiffchen*" seen is gabardine and has artillery buttons.

Three aviators with the rank of *Zugführer* in 1916.

Aviator with the rank of Leutnant in the Balkans in 1916. He does not have a balloon collar insignia, however he has a miniature enamel pilot's badge on his forage cap (*Schiffchen*).

Aviators celebrating Christmas on the eastern front in 1916.

Aviators celebrating Christmas on the southern front. 1917.

A lucky crash landing for the crew of this Br. C I. These aviators wear folding glass *Fliegerbrille* (pilot goggles) which widened their range of sight. Eastern front in 1916.

"*Gut Land*" (Good Landing) was the most difficult for pilots during the First World War. Southern front in 1917.

A snowy field helped soften the landing for this Br. C I. on the eastern front in 1916. Notice the iron crosses on the propellers.

A crash landing of a Br. C I. on the southern front in 1917.

Camouflaged crash landing on the southern front in 1917.

Camouflaged crash landing on the southern front in 1917.

Aviators pause for a photo before take-off. Eastern front. 1916.

Albatross B I, Ba. 22. Southern front 1917.

Br. C I. Southern front. 1917.

Loading bombs into a Lohner B VII, 17.35, "Gral II." Southern front 1917.

A makeshift aircraft hangar on the eastern front in 1916.

Transporting an Av. B III after an emergency landing.

Officer examines the wreckage of an Italian Farman "MF 2657", Type MF II shot down near Maria Gail on April 17, 1917.

Austrian soldiers examining a shot down Italian Farman "MF 2657" Type MF II. 1917.

Gendarme (military police) in summer weight tunic and pith helmet examines the wreckage of a Caudron G III "C 605" shot down on July 4, 1917 near Borgo.

Soldiers of *Infantrie Regiment No. 74* examining the wreckage of a Caproni Ca. 3 shot down on October 27, 1917.

Aviators inflating an observation balloon. Southern front. 1917.

Aviators in the basket of an observation balloon. The shadow of the photographer and his tripod are visible. Southern front. 1917.

Anchoring an observation balloon. Eastern front 1916.

Anchoring an observation balloon. Eastern front 1916.

Pre to early war photo of soldiers transporting an observation balloon up a mountain near Salzburg.

A *celloidin karte* of an aviator in his flight suit. 1917.

Studio photo of an aviator. 1917.

Studio photo of an aviator with the rank of Gefreiter. He wears a private purchase corduroy field tunic with an enamel pilot's badge (*Fliegerabzeichen or Feldpilotabzeichen*) on his right breast pocket. Oddly, he does not wear the balloon collar insignia which is indicative of the aviators. Also, he has been awarded the Kaiser Karl bravery medal in bronze and the Kaiser Karl Truppen Kreuz.

Flight and ground crews pose in front of their Donnet-Leveque Float plane (*Flugboot*) "10". Pola 1916.

Aviators enjoying a drink on the southern front in 1917.

Chapter Five

Anti-Aircraft

10cm anti-aircraft field howitzer (*Fliegerabwehrkannonen)* on the eastern front in 1916. This was essentially a 10cm *Feldhaubitz* mounted on top of large blocks of wood which could be rotated into position.

Anti aircraft cannon (*Fliegerabwehrkannon*) on the eastern front in 1916. Two soldiers alongside operate a field optic. Although large and awkward looking, this optic could be easily dismantled and transported by simply slinging it over ones shoulder like a rifle.

Anti-aircraft cannon *(Fliegerabwehrkannon)* on the eastern front in 1916. This soldier demonstrates how the optic is used. By looking into the center lenses, one could have a wider range of sight through the two lenses on either end.

Anti-aircraft cannon *(Fliegerabwehrkannon)* on the eastern front in 1916.

Anti-aircraft cannon (*Fliegerabwehrkannon*) on the southern front in 1917. Later in the war, this mount was developed making it easier to aim and maneuver.

Anti-aircraft cannon (*Fliegerabwehrkannon*) on the southern front in 1917. Soldier in the middle demonstrates by turning the wheel how the cannon was positioned.

Anti-aircraft cannon (*Fliegerabwehrkannon*) on the southern front in 1917.

A *Schwarzlose* ready to serve as an anti-aircraft gun on the eastern front in 1916.

Aviator posed next to a *Schwarzlose* mounted for use as an anti-aircraft gun. Southern front. 1917.

A Maxim being used as an anti-aircraft gun. Eastern front. 1916.

A captured Maxim -Vickers Model 1911 being used as an anti-aircraft gun in the Dolomites 1917.

Chapter Six

Telefon/Telegraph

This group of soldiers has just completed their *Telegraphenkurs* or telegraph and signal course. Vienna. 1914.

Telegraph and telephone operators on the eastern front.1915

Telephone operators in the trenches on the eastern front. April 26, 1915.

Honvéd (Hungarian) telegraph operators on the eastern front 1916.

Telephone operators on the eastern front 1916. One characteristic of the Austrian field telephone was drop-down sides. This feature provided easy access for repair work.

Signal and telephone troops on the eastern front 1916.

Signal Corps, telephone operators, ulans, dragoons, and hussars. 1917.

Infantrie Regiment No. 27. 1917

Pre to early war telegraph and telephone operators.

Telephone operator with the rank of leutnant on the eastern front. 1916. His holster is for the Roth Steyr Model 1907.

Telephone operator with the rank of Zugführer. 1916

Telephone operators on the eastern front in 1915.

Telephone and telegraph operators on the southern front. 1917. Soldiers in the center have been awarded the bronze bravery medal and the Kaiser Karl Truppen Kreuz.

Telephone and telegraph operators on the eastern front in 1916.

Telegraph operator and infantry private in 1917.

Pre to early war search light (*Scheinwerfer*) troops.

Transporting search lights (*Scheinwerfer*) to the southern front in 1917.

Pre to early war signal corps soldiers.

Telephone operators on the eastern front in 1916.

Telephone operator. 1915

Telephone operator in corduroy. 1916.

A studio photo of a Honvéd (Hungarian) telephone operator in 1917. Numbers on his field cap(tábori sapka) indicate his unit.

Telephone operator in issue uniform. 1917.

Chapter Seven

Edelweiss Collar Insignia *Kaiserschützen*

Studio photo of a *Kaiserschützen* in 1915. The braided cord with five dark green wool balls is a marksmanship cord (*Schützenauszeichnung*).

Kaiserschützen near the southern front in 1917.

Kaiserschützen with M95 *Gewehrs* on the southern front in 1917. Wooden poles on the ground in the snow near some of the troops are walking sticks which help them traverse mountainous terrain.

Studio photo of *Kaiserschützen* in 1916. The two in the front row are holding M95 S*tutzen* and the one in the back row right is wearing the standard issue *Schneebrille* or snow goggles.

Kaiserschützen at a mass in the Dolomites. 1917.

Fortifications on the southern front. 1917.

Soldiers of the *k.u.k. Infantrie Regiment Nr.100.* Kärnten (Carinthia) in 1915.

A studio photo of two enlisted soldiers in issue uniforms. 1917.

Gebirgsjäger engaging the enemy in the Dolomites in 1917.

Kaiserschützen patiently waiting their turn to use an alpine outhouse in 1917.

Studio photo of a *Oberleutnant* wearing his *Oberscharfschützenauszeichnung für Landesschützen mit Signalpfeife which* is a high ranking sharp shooters' cord with a whistle for regional marksmen. 1916.

k.u.k. Standschützen-Baon Innsbruck. 3. Kompagnie on the southern Front in 1917.

Kaiserschützen Nr. 4 in 1914.

k.u.k. Infantrieregiment Erzherzog Rainer Nr. 59. 1917.

A studio photo of *Kaiserschützen* and other enlisted soldiers in 1915.

Gebirgsjäger standing watch in the Dolomites. 1917. Straps on his shoes are for *steigeisen* or iron cleats which made climbing easier.

Kaiserschützen transporting machine guns on the southern front in 1916.

Kaiserschützen on the eastern front in 1915.

Kaiserschützen. 1914.

A studio photo of two *Kaiserschützen*. The soldier on the left wears a *Distanzschätzauszeichnung* or distance judging badge with *1906 Scharfschützenauszeichnung für Jäger und Landwehrfußtruppen* or sharp shooters' cord for the Jäger and Landwehr Infantry. The soldier on the right wears the *1868 Scharfschuetzenauszeichnung für Jäger und Landwehrfusstruppen*. 1915.

Kaiserschützen enjoying a drink during Easter. 1914. Some wear the shortened sabers which were standard issue. Shortened sabers were less cumbersome in mountainous terrain.

Eastern front. 1916.

Two *Kaiserschützen* with the rank of *Gefreiter*. Both wear the *Distanzschaetzauszeichnung* and the *1906 Scharfschutzenauszeichnung für Jäger und Landwehrfusstruppen.*

Tyrolean *Standschützen* from the *k.u.k. Standschützen Baon Innsbruck II*. 1916.

Kaiserschützen enjoying a drink in 1916.

Kaiserschützen in 1915. In the center sits a general major.

Kaiserschützen enjoying a meal in the Dolomites in 1917.

Pre to early war troops on ski patrol.

Korporal. 1916.

Kaiserschützen in private purchase pressed felt cap and lambs fur lined leather coat. Southern front. 1917.

Ski patrol. 1915.

Maneuvers. 1915.

Kaiserschützen on ski patrol in 1916.

A studio photo *Kaiserschützen* in issue *Feldmütze*, private purchase wool tunic and gabardine pants. 1917.

Kaiserschützen in ersatz tunic and pants in 1918. He has been awarded the silver bravery medal 1st class.

Kaiserschützen on the eastern front in 1916.

Kaiserschützen on the eastern front in 1916. Soldier on the left with the rank of *Korporal* wears a *Distanzschaetzauszeichnung* and a *1868 Scharfschuetzenauszeichnung für Jäger und Landwehrfusstruppen*. Soldier on the right with the rank of *Zugsführer* wears the *1906 Scharfschutzenauszeichnung für Jäger and Landwehrfusstruppen.*

Kaiserschützen. 1915.

Kaiserschützen. 1917.

Kaiserschützen in issue tunic and pants. His hat is a privately purchased pressed felt field cap and he carries an ersatz or *not* bayonet.

*Kaiserschützen (*right) and enlisted soldier (left).

A studio photo of a *Kaiserschützen*. 1916.

A studio photo of a *Kaiserschützen*. He has a cloth machinegunner insignia embellished with gold thread stitched to his left sleeve. 1916.

A studio photo of a *Kaiserschützen* in a classic issue uniform. 1917.

A studio photo of a *Kaiserschützen*. 1916.

A studio photo of a *Kaiserschützen*. 1915.

A studio photo of a *Leutnant* wearing his A*usgangskäppi* with Kaiser Karl cockade and his Karl's *bluse*. He has been awarded the gilded Kaiser Karl military service medal 1st class, the Kaiser Karl bravery medal in silver 2nd class and the Kaiser Karl Truppen Kreuz. Vienna 1918.

Chapter Eight

Dragoons

Pre to early war photo of Dragoons. The two dragoons on the far left and right wear the *Dragonermannschaftshelm Model 1850* or the Dragoons helmet for enlisted soldiers Model 1850.

Dragoons. 1914.

Dragoon wearing *Dragonermannschaftshelm Model 1850.* He carries the M95 Carbine. Cavalry used single ammo pouches.

This dragoon wears the *Schützenauszeichnung für die Kavallerie* which is marksman badge for Cavalry and the 1906 *Reiterauszeichnung* or rider's badge.

Dragoons trying to free an officer's car from the mud on the eastern front.1915.

Dragoons in 1915. Some have been awarded the Kaiser Franz Joseph's Jubilee Cross. Displayed front and center is a saddle, blanket, bridle, bugle and two carbines. Dragoons on the left and right wear the *Dragonermannschaftshelm Model 1850*. Single ammo pouches were typical for the cavalry.

k.u.k. Dragoner Regiment Nr. 6 *Instruktionskader* or Instruction Cadre. Most are wearing an instructor's whistle. Vienna. 1915.

k.u.k. Dragoner Regiment Friederich August König von Sachsen Nr. 3. 1915

A Dragoon on the eastern front. 1914.

A studio photo of a Dragoon and a machine gunner both of whom are enlisted soldiers. 1915.

Eastern front. 1915.

Dragoon Officer. 1914. He wears the *Dragoneroffiziershelm Model 1850.*

Dragoons on the eastern front in 1915.

Dragoons in Vienna in 1914. Most wear the *Schützenauszeichnung für Kavallerie* or marksman badge for cavalry and the *Reiterauszeichnung* or rider Badge. On display in the center between the two buglers are a saddle and bridles.

Studio photo of a Dragoon in 1915. Leather pommel on his sword was for NCOs or Unteroffiziers.

A lady poses for a picture in a *Dragonerunteroffiziershelm model 1850*, an *unteroffizierskartusche* (NCOs ammunition pouch), and *unteroffiziersabel* (NCOs sword). Vienna. 1914.

Dragoons in Austria in 1914. Most wear the *Schutzenauszeichnungen für Kavallerie*, *Reiterauszeichungen* and service crosses.

Studio photo of a dragoon in the *Model 1850 Dragonerhelm.* Vienna 1915.

A studio photo of a dragoon and two infantry soldiers. 1915.

A studio photo of a dragoon wearing the Franz Joseph I Jubilee medal. Infantry soldiers are also present. 1915.

Studio photo of a dragoon in 1915. He wears an edelweiss on his red cavalry forage cap and wears a classic cavalry boot with spurs mounted into the heel. Not all cavalry had this type of boot. There were also depot-stamped issue spurs with leather straps which buckled around the heel and instep.

Studio photo of a dragoon. He wears the *Schützenauszeichnung für die Kavallerie* and a *Reiterauszeichnung*. He has the rank of *Korporal*.

Chapter Nine

Hussars

Pre to early war photo of Hussars. This particular studio photo was taken in Temesvár located the former region of the Empire known as the Banat. The Banat was a multiethnic region largely settled by Danube Swabians (*Donau Schwaben*) and Hungarians (*Magyar*).

Pre to early war photos of Hussars.

Hussars. 1915.

Hussar. 1914.

Chapter Ten

Ulans

A studio photo of an *Oberleutnant* of the ulans. 1914.

A studio photo of the enlisted soldiers of the ulans. 1915.

Studio photo of an ulan with the rank *Korporal* in Oberhollabrunn in 1915.

Ulans ready to leave for the eastern front in 1915.

Ulans riding through an Austrian town on the way to the eastern front in 1915.

Ulans riding through an Austrian town on the way to the eastern front in 1915.

Ulans awaiting inspection from the *Generalstab* or General staff on the eastern front.1915.

Ulans shodding their horses on the eastern front in 1915.

Ulans. 1914.

Ulans on the eastern front 1915. Ulan on the left has the rank of Zugführer and carries a Roth Steyr Model 1907.

Chapter Eleven

Motor Corps
Kraftfahrzeug und Kraftfahrer

Kraftfahrer 1914/15

Kraftfahrer on the eastern front in 1916. The *Kraftfahrer* wore leather as opposed to wool because they were more exposed to the elements. Particularly prized by the *Kraftfahrer* was the *leder feldmuetze* or leather field cap.

Soldiers of the *k.u.k. Armee-Kraftwagenwerkstaette Nr. 8.* or royal and imperial Army Motor Corp Repair Station in 1917.

A studio photo of a *Kraftfahrer* with the rank of *Oberleutnant* in 1916. He wears the *Autolenkerauszeichung* or Driver's Badge.

Kraftfahrer on the southern front in 1917. Soldier on the right wears a leather field cap, while the one in the middle wears a leather hat normally worn by volunteers, and the soldier on the left wears a private purchase pressed felt hat.

Kraftfahrer on the eastern front in 1916.

Officer of a *Kraftfahrer Korps* on the southern front in 1917.

Kraftfahrer from the *k.u.k. Infantrie Regiment Freiherr von Hess Nr. 49*. 1917.

Kraftfahrer enjoying wine from the vineyards in Latisana in 1917

Kraftfahrer on the eastern front in 1916.

Kraftfahrer in a repair shop. 1916.

This Hussar has traded in his horse for an armored car (*Panzer auto*). Eastern front. 1916.

Kraftfahrer on the eastern front. 1915.

A studio photo of a *Kraftfahrer* and his wife. 1917

An Austrian *Kraftfahrzeug*, which has been fitted to run on train tracks, taking Germans to the eastern front. 1915.

Kraftfahrer pose for a photo before departing for the eastern front in 1915.

Changing a wheel on the eastern front in 1916.

A partially disassembled *Kraftfahrzeug*. Eastern front. 1916.

Kraftfahrer on the eastern front in 1915. On the left is a general purpose utility wagon.

An inspection from *Erzherzog Friederich* in Huszt.

Erzherzog Albrecht with *Rittmeister Graf Thun* in Marmomarosz-Sziget.

Front and rear views of the *Zugwagen M. 12/16*, taken from a 1918 maintenance manual issued to the *Kraftfahrer* . This vehicle was used to tow heavy artillery.

Side view of the *Zugwagen M.* 12/16, taken from a 1918 maintenance manual issued to the *Kraftfahrer*. This vehicle was used to tow heavy artillery.

Stopping to take in the breath taking mountain scenery on the southern front. Soldier in the center standing in front of the tire is a *gendarme* (military policeman) with the rank of *feldwebel*. He wears the summer weight khaki pith helmet, normally made of cork. 1916

Chapter Twelve

Medical

Feld Lazarett or field hospital on the eastern front in 1915

The transport seen here was used for moving severely wounded soldiers in mountainous terrain. Balkans. 1916

Feld Lazarett or field hospital on the eastern front in 1916.

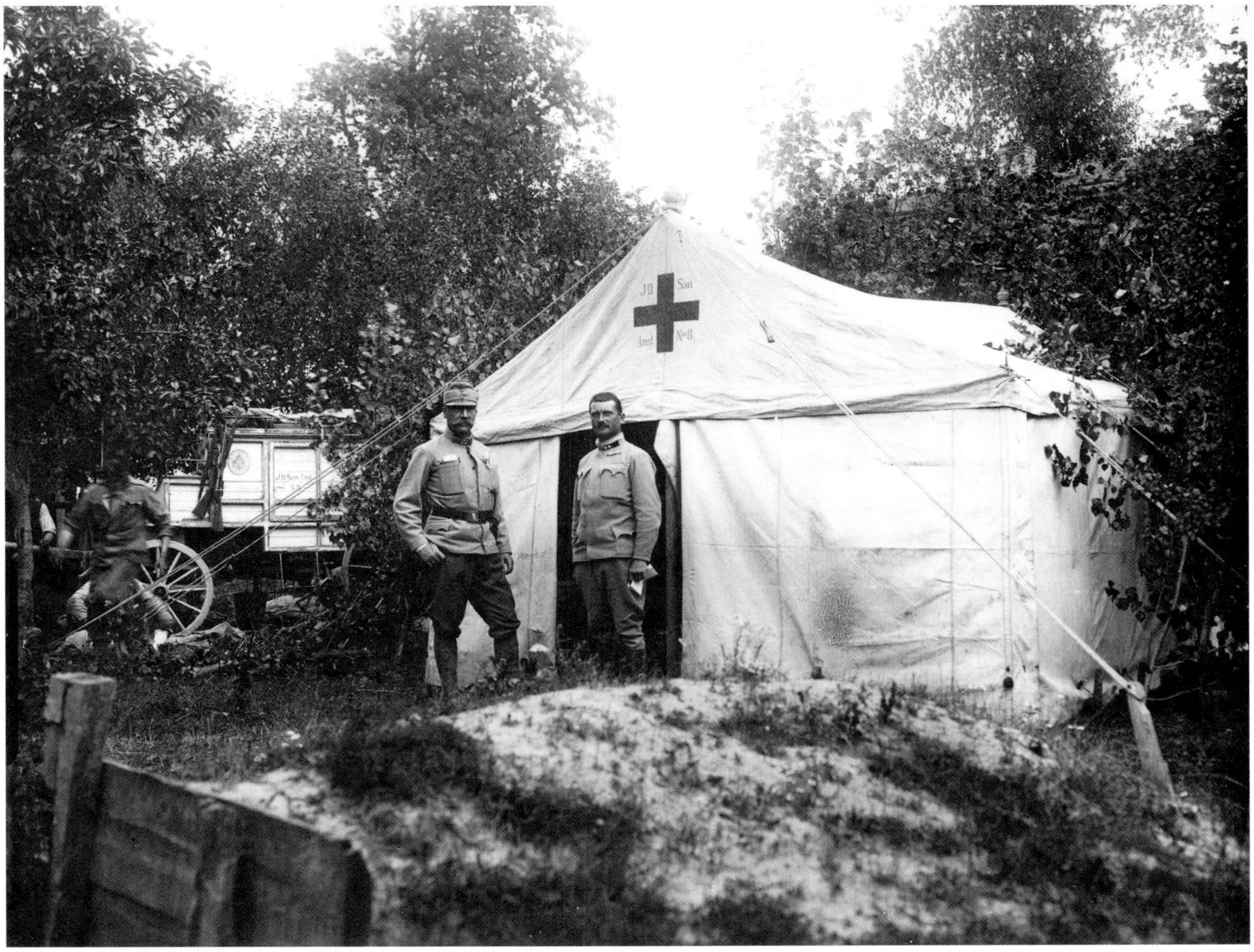

Two officers from the 9th Korps visiting the *Jäger Division Sanitäts Anstalt Nr. 8* or the Jäger Division Medical Establishment Nr. 8. 1916.

Feld Lazarett or field hospital for the 15 *Kompanie*. 1916.

Baon Hilfplatz or Battalion field hospital on the eastern front 1916.

Truck Nr. 7 of the *k.u.k Sanitätsautokolonne* or Mobil Medical Convoy Nr. 8. 1916.

Medical supply wagons on the eastern front in 1916.

A *schlafwagen* or sleeping car which has been converted into a hospital. The medic wears two armbands. One armband has a red cross and the other a Maltese cross from the Knights of Malta. The Knights of Malta assisted in caring for the wounded. Eastern front. 1916.

Mobil Medical Convoy. 1915.

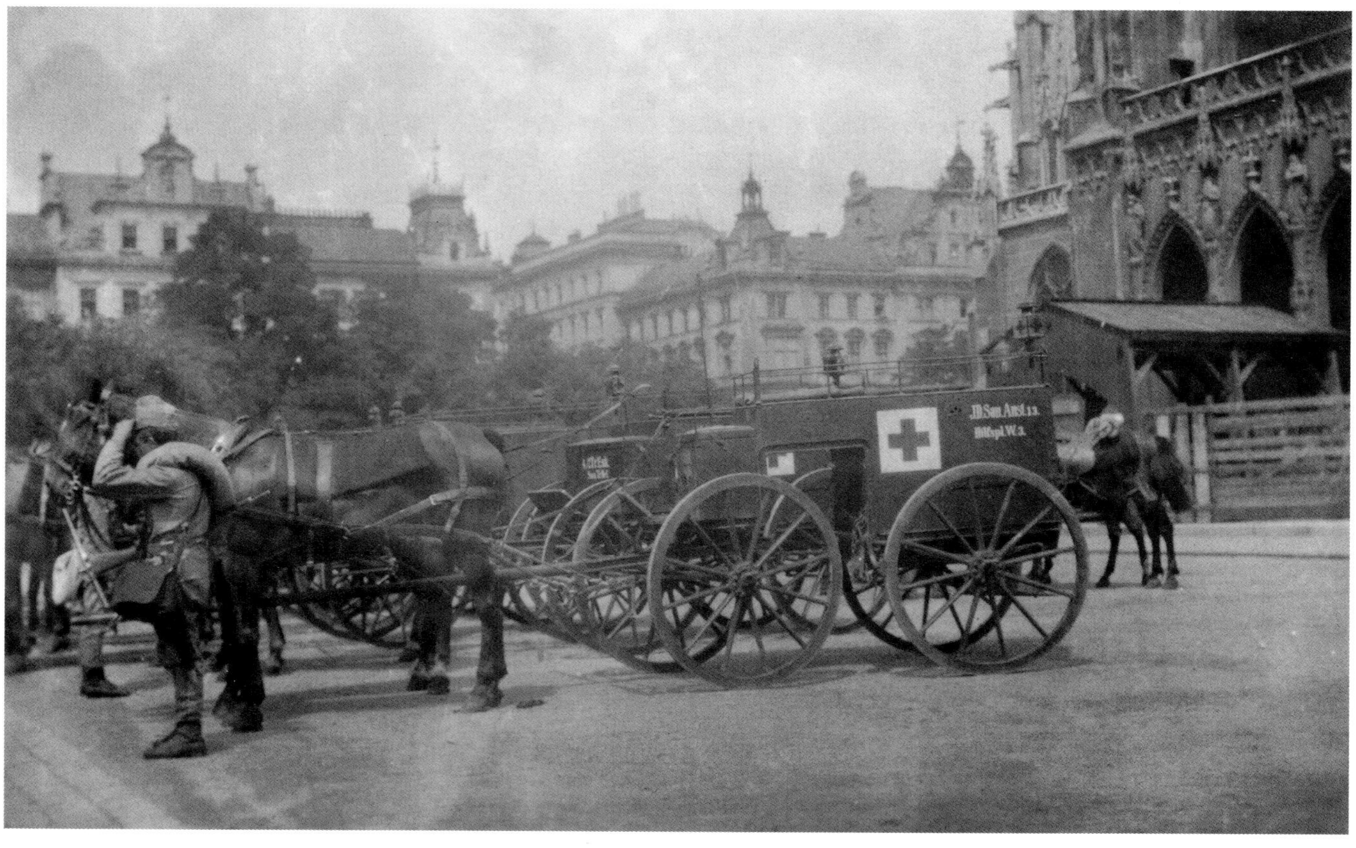

Medical supply wagons. 1915

Feld Lazarett or field hospital on the southern front. 1917

Feld Lazarett or Field Hospital . 1915. Sitting first and second row center are Bosnians in field gray (*feldgrau*) fezzes.

Medical supply wagons on the eastern front in 1915.

Nurses of the *Österreiches Rotes Kreuz* or Austrian Red Cross on the eastern front in 1915

Medical supply wagons on the eastern front in 1916.

Medical supply wagons on the eastern front in 1916.

Lazarett. Vienna. 1914

Medic. 1916

Chapter Thirteen

Austrian Stahlhelms and Berndorfers

Soldiers from the *k.u.k Schützenregiment Nr. 21*. All have received the Silver Bravery Medal 1st class. Soldier in middle is a *Stabsfeldwebel* or drill instructor as his whistle indicates. 1917.

Sturmtruppen or assault Troops in the Dolomites in 1917. Soldier in middle wears winter camouflage over his field gray (*feldgrau*).

Oberjäger from the *k.u.k Schützenregiment Nr. 21*. April 7, 1917.

Southern front. 1917.

Bergführer or mountain guides on the Isonzo front. 1917. Most are wearing *Berndorfer* helmets which were of Austrian design and manufacture. Besides its distinctive shape, the *Berndorfer* had a vent on top. Also, these *Bergführer* have a *stoff* or cloth *Bergführer* patch on their left arms.

Sturmtruppen in Berndorfers on the southern front in 1918.

Soldier of the *k.u.k Infantrie Regiment Freiherr von Succovaty Nr. 87*. This photo was taken on Mount Saint Gabriele on the Isonzo front in May 1917.

Southern front. July 13, 1918.

Southern front. 1916. The soldier on the right has been awarded the silver bravery medal 2nd class and the bronze bravery medal. The next soldier has been awarded the gold bravery medal, silver bravery medal 1st and 2nd class and the bronze bravery medal. The soldier on the left has been awarded silver bravery medal 1st and 2nd class. All have a crossed shovel cloth insignia. The black arm band is in honor of the Kaiser's death.

k.u.k Infantrie Regiment Freiherr von Drathschmidt Nr. 101. All pictured here have won bravery medals. 1917.

Southern front. 1917.

Officers visiting troops on the southern front in 1917.

German and Austrian *Generalstab* or general staff visiting the front in 1916.

These troops show they are ready for whatever awaits them on the Isonzo front in 1917.

After a bombardment on the southern front in 1917.

Chapter Fourteen

Bosnians

Balkans. 1915. Front row right is a Bosnian in a field gray fez.

Bosnian troops in field gray fezzes awaiting an inspection from Kaiser Karl on the southern front in 1917.

Balkans. 1916. Bosnian in a red fez with the rank of *Zugführer*. He has been awarded several bravery medals.

Bosnian musician. 1916.

In a *Lazarett* outside the nurses' station, a *Zugführer* in a red fez looks on while his comrade receives special medical attention.

Southern front. 1916. This photo displays the various shapes of fezzes (cylindrical and conical) as well as the various colors (red and field gray).

Balkans. 1915.

Lazarett. 1915.

Lazarett. 1916.

A staged or mock combat shot of pre to early war soldiers.

"In memory of the first the of the war-1914"

Southern front. 1916.

A highly decorated Bosnian unit poses for a group photo. All of their fezzes are field gray and all appear to have won the silver bravery medal 2nd class or a bronze bravery medal. 1916

Bosnian unit at rest on the southern front. 1916

Austrians and Bosnians atop a mountain knoll in the Balkans in 1916.

Bosnians enjoying a meal. *Kappeabzeichen* (cap badges) were worn on the fezzes as well. An Austrian can also be seen in the background. Balkans 1916.

A highly decorated Bosnian unit. The second soldier on the right side in the second row from the top shows how *Kappeabzeichen* (cap badges) were popular with all soldiers in the *k.u.k.* forces. Two of these soldiers seated in the first row have also won the silver bravery medal 1st class. This photo also shows a nice mixture of red and *feldgrau* fezzes. Balkans 1916

A studio photo of Bosnians in *feldgrau*. 1915

A highly decorated Bosnian unit. Many have been awarded the silver bravery medal both 1st and 2nd class as well as the bronze bravery medal.

Austrian and Bosnian troops send an "*Östergrusse vom Felde* 1915" or "Easter greetings from the front 1915" back home. Balkans 1916.

Chapter Fifteen

Railroad/Eisenbahn

Panzerzug or armored train on the eastern front in 1916.

Eisenbahn troops in 1917. *Zugführer* in the middle wears a private purchase corduroy tunic.

Panzerzug or armored train on the eastern front in 1915.

Eisenbahnpioneere or railroad pioneers. 1916.

Pre to early war *eisenbahn* troops.

Southern front. 1915.

Panzerzug or armored train on the eastern front in 1916

Panzerzug or armored train on the eastern front. in 1916.

Feldwebel. 1917.

Eastern front. 1915.

Southern front. 1917.

Chapter Sixteen

General Infantry and Other Ranks

Gefreiter wearing artillerist cordage (*Vormeister-schnurr) and* carrying a Russian bayonet for the Nagant rifle. 1916.

In this 1917 studio photo three different types of goggles (*brille*) can be seen.

Summer on the eastern front in 1916. The two soldiers lying in front display captured Russian Nagant rifles, while the soldier directly behind the one on the left wears a captured Russian bayonet for the Nagant rifle. The two soldiers in the center of the last row are wearing cloth belts.

A Studio photo of a *Bergführer* (Mountain Patrol Leader) with the rank of Korporal. 1917. He has been awarded the Kaiser Karl bravery medal in bronze as well as the *Kaiser Karl Truppen Kreuz*. On his left sleeve, half of a *Bergführer* patch can be seen. The entire patch consists of a "B" and "F" with a mountain pick in the middle of the two letters.

NCO proudly posed with his captured Russian bayonet. 1916

Late fall on the Russian front in 1915.

Eastern Tyrolean (*Ost Tiroler*) troops in 1917. The soldier standing on the right wears a *grabendolch* (trench knife).

Studio photo of a *Honvéd szakaszvezeto (*platoon leader) in *Pelzrock* (fur lined coat) and *Honvéd Pantalon* or *Magyarnadrág* (Hungarian britches). He wears a wool, rolled stocking cap without cockade which was popular with the troops, particularly those serving in cold climates. 1916.

A studio photo of a *Zugführer* with an 8mm *Rast and Gasser*. 1916.

An enlisted soldier in classic issue *feldgrau*. Vienna. 1916.

Soldier of *k.u.k Graf von Khevenhueller Nr. 7*. He holds an M95 *Gewehr* and is wearing an early style *Kalbsfelltornister* (calfskin backpack). 1915.

A studio photo of an enlisted soldier. He holds an M95*Gewehr* and wears an ersatz belt with an unusual style of ammo pouch. 1917.

Two soldiers of enlisted rank pose for a studio photo before leaving for the front in 1916. Both wear classic issue uniforms and equipment.

These troops stand ready with their grenades in their well-camouflaged trenches on the southern front. Autumn 1916.

A group of battle-hardened soldiers of the *k.u.k Landsturm Infantrie Baon Nr. 172, 2. Kompanie*. December 9, 1916.

Wagons for carrier pigeons (*breiftauben*). Pigeons played a vital role in communication and information gathering. Cameras were even developed which could be attached to the breast of the pigeon to obtain aerial photographs. Southern front 1916.

Trench line on the eastern front in 1915.

This studio photo displays a variety of uniforms and decorations. The *Zugführer*, *Korporal*, and *Gefreiter* have all been awarded the iron cross 2nd class. The *Gefreiter* has also won the silver bravery medal 1st class. Graz 1917.

Soldiers of the *Landsturm Infantrie Regiment Wien Nr. 1* receiving decorations on the eastern front. 1916.

Soldiers of the *k.u.k Schützen Regiment Nr. 7 Jagdkommando*. Soldier in the center has been awarded the silver bravery medal 2nd and the bronze bravery medal. 1917.

A fantastic display of edged weaponry, field telephones, and *Schwarzlose MG*. In the center sits a *beamter* (civil servant), to the right in the second row is an Ulan and to the left and right with edelweiss on their collars are *Kaiserschützen*. Balkans 1915.

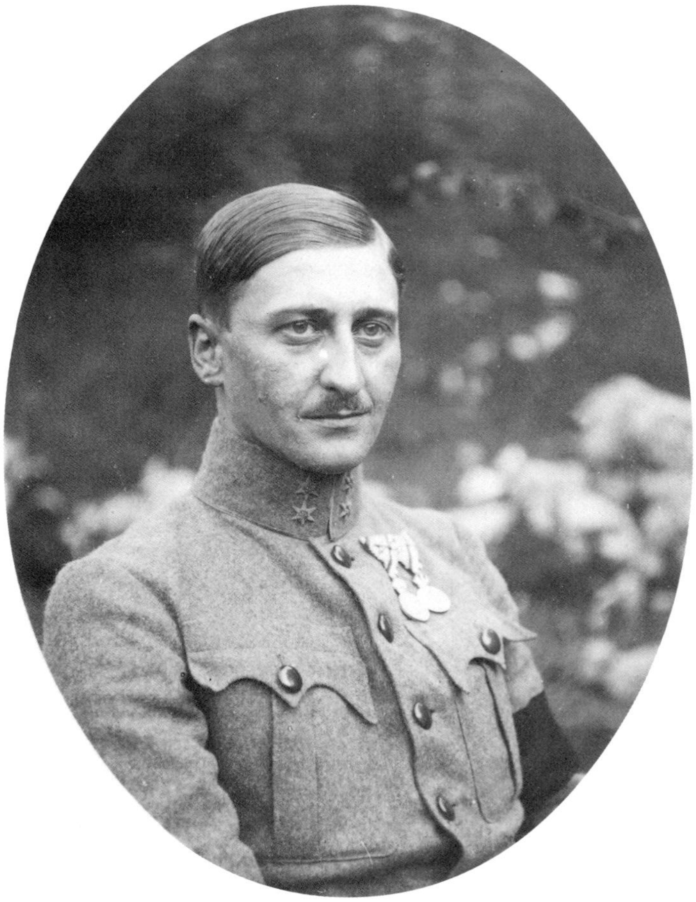

This *Oberleutnant is* wearing a *Karl's bluse*. The black band on his arm is in honor of the deceased Kaiser Franz Joseph I. He has been awarded the silver and bronze military service crosses with swords. 1916.

A studio photo of a *Honved.* He wears the classic *honved pantalon* or *Magyarnadrág* (Hungarian britches) and on his field cap (*tábori sapka*) an IFJ cockade. 1916

A studio photo of an enlisted man in a fur-lined tunic (*Pelzrock*). Vienna 1915.

A studio photo of a *Zugführer*. He has been awarded a small enamel Franz Joseph I service cross, Franz Joseph service cross in iron, and a mobilization cross. Vienna 1915.

Ski patrol on the southern front on February 2, 1915

This photo shows the various types of *ledergamaschen* (leather gaiters) available. Vienna 1917.

Ski troops of enlisted rank ready to embark for the southern front. Soldier on the left carries a *stutzen* and fastened atop his backpack are snowshoes (scheeschue). This picture was taken in Graz in 1916.

Oberst and *Regiment Kommandant* of the *k.u.k Infantrie Regiment Hoch und Deutschmeister Nr. 4.* On his private purchase pressed felt field cap is an enamel on silver *Hoch und Deutschmeister* regimental cap badge. In addition to others medals, he has also been awarded the German Iron Cross 2nd class.

This *Oberstleutnant* has been award the Iron Cross 2nd class, the *Eisernen Krone* (Iron Crown) 3rd class and an enameled military service cross. Graz. 1917.

This *Oberleutnant* has been awarded the Kaiser Franz Joseph silver with red enamel service cross 1st and 2nd class as well as the military jubilee cross. Vienna 1916.

An enlisted soldier on the southern front in 1916. Tucked between his bread-bag strap and mantel are a pair of winter mittens. The holes and markings burned into the wooden handle of his pick axe *(Beilpicke)* are measuring or detailing indicator holes (*Zentimetereinteilung*).

A studio photo of enlisted men in issue uniforms. The roll on the end of their right shoulder epaulette held the *Gewehr riemen* or gun sling in place while marching. Graz 1915

Two gendarme, staff officers (*Stabsoffiziere)*, high-ranking officers (*Oberoffiziere)* and NCOs (*Unteroffiziere)* in Villach in 1916. The three soldiers on the left wear the black armband in honor of the deceased Kaiser Franz Joseph I.

Enlisted men in issue uniforms with M95 *Gewehrs*. Collar covers kept the wool tunic from rubbing their necks sore. Vienna 1916

Studio photo of an enlisted man. *Mantel* or overcoat, *feldmütze* and wool gaiters are issue. He wears his *Beilpicke* (pick-axe) behind his bayonet and to the left of his rucksack according *Vorschriften*(regulations manual). The *Beilpicke* consisted of a *Hacke* or axe and a *Pickel* or pick and was used for small demolition work. It could cut through a tree with a 30 cm trunk and was issued normally to every tenth soldier. This soldier has his mess tin strapped on to a pair of snowshoes (*scheeschue*). Salzburg 1915.

An enlisted soldier on the eastern front in 1915. He wears the infantry shovel (*Infantriespaten)* according to regulations (*Vorschriften*). The *Infantriespaten* was made of cast steel (*Gußstahl)* and the handle was made of ash wood (*Eschenholz)*.

A *Zugführer* on the eastern front in 1915. On his private purchase pressed felt hat are an edelweiss and a Franz Joseph I with laurel leaves cap badge (*kappe abzeichen*).

Pre to early war photo of an enlisted soldier. He wears an early style *Kalbsfelltornister* (calfskin backpack), ammo pouch, and gaiter.

A studio photo of a *Zugführer* taken in Pola (a k.u.k Naval Base) in 1915. He wears the holster and 8mm round ammo pouch for the *Rast and Gasser* M. 98.

An enlisted soldier with an M95 *Gewehr*. This photo was taken in Prague in 1915.

Zugführer in the Dolomites in 1917. He carries a *stutzen* and wears Pre to early war ammo pouches. He has been awarded the silver bravery medal 2nd class and the military jubilee medal. Between the two buttons on his *feldmütze* he wears a red and white enamel U-boot *abzeichen*. The k.u.k Navy (k.u.k *Kriegsmarine)* was very popular with soldiers in all branches of the *k.u.k.* military. Purchasing this particular *abzeichen* helped support the *Kriegs Waisen und Witwe* or War Orphans and Widows.

A *feldwebel* and *Korporal* on the eastern front in 1915. Both wear issue *ledergamaschen* and carry a Roth Steyr Model 1907.

A studio photo of four *Unteroffiziere*. *Feldwebel* on the right wears a private purchase pair of lace-up boots. The sign in the center reads "In memory of Christmas 1914 in Johansdorf." This photo was taken in Schoenberg.

A studio photo of two enlisted soldiers ready to head for the front in 1915. Both wear the early style *Kalbsfelltornister* (calfskin backpack). Innsbruck. 1915.

Soldiers of the *k.u.k Ersatzbataillon Nr. 11*. The two *Unteroffiziere* in the photo carry issue shortened sabers which made maneuvering in the trenches and mountainous terrain less cumbersome. Several soldiers have also been awarded bravery medals.

An enlisted soldier in summer weight uniforms carrying stutzen. Vienna 1915.

A studio photo of two enlisted soldiers 1915.

Chapter Seventeen

Dog Transport Teams Hundertraingespann

Dog transport team on the eastern front in 1915

Dog transport team of the *k.u.k Infantrie Regiment Ritter von Auffenberg Nr. 64*. 1916.

Dog transport team hauling firewood on the southern front in 1917

Feeding time for the dogs on the southern front. 1917

Dog transport team hauling food supplies for the troops on the southern front in 1917.

Training center for dogs transport teams.

Warehouse for *Hundewagon* or wagons for the transport dogs .

Dog transport team in front of a field hospital near the southern front in 1917.

Dog transport team. 1917

Chapter Eighteen

Kaiser Jäger

A group of Kaiser Jäger pose for a photo in 1916. Several have been awarded bravery medals.

Three Kaiser Jäger with the rank of *Zugführer* and *k.u.k.* Infantry in Graz in 1915.

A studio photo of pre to early war Tyrolean Kaiser Jäger.

Tyrolean Kaiser Jäger with the rank of Fähnrich. Brunn. January 19, 1917.

Kaiser Jäger with the rank of *Leutnant*. August 30, 1917.

Pre to early war Kaiser Jäger.

Pre to early war studio photo of a Tyrolean Kaiser Jäger with the rank of *Korporal*. He wears the *Scharfschützenauszeichnung für Jäger* or sharp shooters' decoration.

A studio photo of a Tyrolean Kaiser Jäger with the rank of *Leutnant*.

Kaiser Jäger with the rank of *Fähnrich* in a summer weight *Karl's Bluse*. Southern front 1917.

Kaiser Jäger with the rank of *Hauptmann* in private purchase leather gaiters (*Ledergemaschen*). Southern front 1917.

Kaiser Jäger with the rank of *Oberleutnant*. He wears a *Karl's Bluse* and has been awarded a bravery medal. This photo was taken in Steyr on September 1, 1917.

A studio photo of Kaiser Jäger taken January 23, 1915 in Feldkirch. Soldier in the center and soldier on the right have the rank of *Fähnrich.* Soldier on the left has the rank of *Leutnant*. The soldiers look as though they are preparing for a cold winter the front.

Two Kaiser Jäger in overcoats (*Mantel*). Kaiser Jäger on the right wears a *feldgrau Mantel mit Pelzkragen* or field gray overcoat with fur collar. Kaiser Jäger on the left wear a *hechtgrau mantel mit Samt Kragen* or pike/blue gray overcoat with velvet collar.

Chapter Nineteen

Ersatz/Private Purchase/Unusual

A studio photo of an enlisted rank soldier in an issue field gray (*feldgrau*) uniform. He wears a pair of privately purchased mountain boots (*Bergschue*).

An enlisted rank soldier in ersatz tunic and belt. His *feldmütze* is original issue. Many ersatz uniforms were made out of materials which could be *ausgekocht* or boiled to prevent the spread of diseases. Graz. 1918

A *Fähnrich* on the southern front in 1917. He wears a summer weight uniform and has been awarded the bronze bravery medal, the Kaiser Franz Joseph I service cross made of iron and the *Kaiser Karl Truppen Kreuz.*

Three enlisted rank soldiers in issue uniforms and carrying ersatz bayonets. Villach 1917.

Three soldiers of enlisted rank from the *Telefon Abteilung Nr. 17* on the south western front in 1916. Soldier on the left carries a *Stutzen* and wears a knitted wool, rolled stocking cap (*Mütze*) with cockade. Soldier in the center wears telegraph/telefon collar insignia and carries a Roth Steyr Model 1907. Soldier on the right also wears the knitted wool, rolled stocking cap (*Mütze*). His *Mütze* has two decorative non-functional buttons.

This photo of enlisted soldiers was taken at a *kaserne* or barracks near Vienna in 1917.

This enlisted rank soldier wears a private purchase pressed felt *Feldmütze* with a polished black stone and a silver patriotic cap badges (*Kappeabzeichen)* depicting Kaiser Franz Joseph I, and a fur-lined tunic (*Pelzrock*). 1917.

A studio photo of an enlisted rank soldier in a late war ersatz field tunic (*Feld Bluse*). This *Feld Bluse* no longer has the traditional scalloped pocket flap. Also visible on this *Feld Bluse* is the waist drawstring which can be found on earlier *Feldblusen* as well. Klagenfurt. 1918.

A studio photo of two enlisted rank soldiers of the *k.u.k. Infantrie Regiment Freiherr von Bolfras Nr. 84*. 1917

A studio photo of a *Korporal* in a knitted wool, rolled stocking *Mütze* with an FJI cockade and decorative buttons. Graz. 1916.

A studio photo of a *Feldwebel*. His *Feldmütze* is very unusual in that it has round shape and a wool covered visor. 1916.

This group photo dated 1915 shows pre to early war as well as mid to late war uniforms. The enlisted soldier sitting on the right end of the bench carries an ersatz bayonet. Others in the group wear ersatz belts.

A studio photo of five enlisted soldiers and a *Zugführer*. Particularly interesting is the conical shape of the field caps (*Feldmütze)* these soldiers are wearing. The sign in the center reads." In memory of the mobilization in 1914."

A studio photo of an enlisted soldier. He wears an issue uniform made of *wuschelig* or fuzzy wool. This photo is dated 1916.

A studio photo of an *Oberleutnant* in his summer uniform. 1918

A studio photo taken in Linz in 1916. This photo displays the many interpretations of the overcoat collar or *Mantel Kragen* such as fur (*Pelz*) or velvet (*Samt*). The soldier on the ground in front on the left with the rank of *Gefreiter* wears an issue fuzzy or *wuschelig* wool field tunic *Feld Bluse*.

A studio photo of enlisted soldiers. The soldier sitting on the bench to the left carries an ersatz bayonet while the soldier on the right carries a Russian bayonet.

This soldier wears a private purchase corduroy *Feld Bluse* and is holding his private purchase pressed felt *Feldmütze*. Also, he has been awarded the *Kaiser Karl Truppen Kreuz*. 1917.

Enlisted rank soldier wearing an ersatz belt and bayonet frog. 1917

A group photo taken in Nieder Österreich in 1916. Many of the enlisted soldiers in this photo wear ersatz belts.

A group photo taken in 1917. Many of the enlisted soldiers wear single ersatz ammo pouches made out of lead or *Kriegsmetall* with a leather fastening strap. Soldier lying in the front on the right wears a Russian bayonet.

A studio photo of a *Zugführer* in a summer weight *Karl's Bluse* with interior buttons. His forage cap *(Schiffchen)* is made of a fuzzy wool. Eisenstadt 1917.

An enlisted man on the western front in 1917. He carries a M95 Gewehr and an *Infantriespaten*. He wears a standard issue uniform and ersatz ammo pouches. Ersatz pouches were made of either lead, *Kriegsmetall* or vulcanized cardboard.

Three *Gefreiter* from a *Sturm Halbbaon* (Assault Half Battalion) on the southern front 1918. All three have been awarded bravery medals. Between the buttons of their *Feldmütze* is an assault troops (*Sturmtruppen)* badge depicting skull and crossed grenades.

A photo of two *Zugführer* and six enlisted soldiers taken in Innsbruck, April 11, 1915. All wear the knitted wool rolled stocking cap (*Mütze*).

A *Leutnant* in *Pelzmantel* with a map case or (*Kartentaschen*). His boots are private purchase. The felt part of the boot can be rolled up over the knee for more protection in harsh weather conditions.

A group photo of enlisted soldiers (*Mannschaft*) and NCOs (*Unteroffiziere*) wearing ersatz belts. 1917.

A studio photo of enlisted soldiers taken in Vienna in 1917. Except for the seated soldier on the left, all wear late war ersatz tunics.

An enlisted soldier in an ersatz tunic with standing collar. This tunic has straight-cut pocket flaps instead of scallop cut. His *Feldmütze* appears to be issue. Graz. 1918.

A studio photo of a *Feuerwerker* in 1917. *Feuerwerker* is the name of the rank of a soldier attached to artillery units and is roughly the equivalent of *Feldwebel*. This *Feuerwerker* wears an ersatz tunic. His small brass buttons with crossed cannons indicate he is attached to an artillery unit.

A studio photo of a *Leutnant* and an enlisted man in knitted wool, rolled stocking cap *Mütze*. *Leutnant* wears issue leather gaiters or *Ledergemaschen*. March 1, 1915.

A studio photo of an enlisted man with ersatz belt and bayonet frog.

A studio photo of a *Gefreiter* in ersatz tunic and private purchase pressed felt *Feldmütze*. 1917

A studio photo of three enlisted soldiers. All three wear the sharp shooters' cord for the Infantry (*Scharfschützenauszeichnung für die Infantrie)* and carry ersatz bayonets.

A studio photo of an enlisted soldier wearing an ersatz belt. Feldkirch, Vorarlberg. 1917

A studio photo of a soldier in the *k.u.k Infantrie Regiment Nr. 93*. His field cap (*Feldmütze*) has an unusual shape and is most likely private purchase. October 29, 1918

A studio photo of enlisted soldiers wearing issue uniforms and carrying ersatz bayonets. Graz 1917.

A studio photo of an enlisted soldier wearing an ersatz belt and bayonet frog. Vienna 1918.

An enlisted rank soldier in a knitted wool rolled stocking cap *(Mütze)* and a fur lined overcoat (*pelz gefuttert Mantel*) on the Eastern front in 1915.

A studio photo of a *Leutnant* wearing an *Ausgangskäppi* and an overcoat (*Mantel*) with a *Samt Kragen* or velvet collar.

A studio of a *Feldwebel* and his dog. He wears a private purchase *feldmütze* with a Kaiser Karl cockade and commercial celluloid buttons. The number 13 indicates the unit to which he was attached. This photo was taken in Vienna in 1916.

Chapter Twenty

Artillery and Artillerists

A 10cm *Feldhaubitz* M14 or field cannon in a camouflaged firing position on the eastern front 1915.

A 10cm *Feldhaubitz* M14 on the southern front in 1917. The seven crew members stand ready with their gas masks in case of a gas attack.

A 10cm *Feldhaubitz* M14 on an eastern front road in 1915.

A 10 cm *Feldhaubitz* M14.

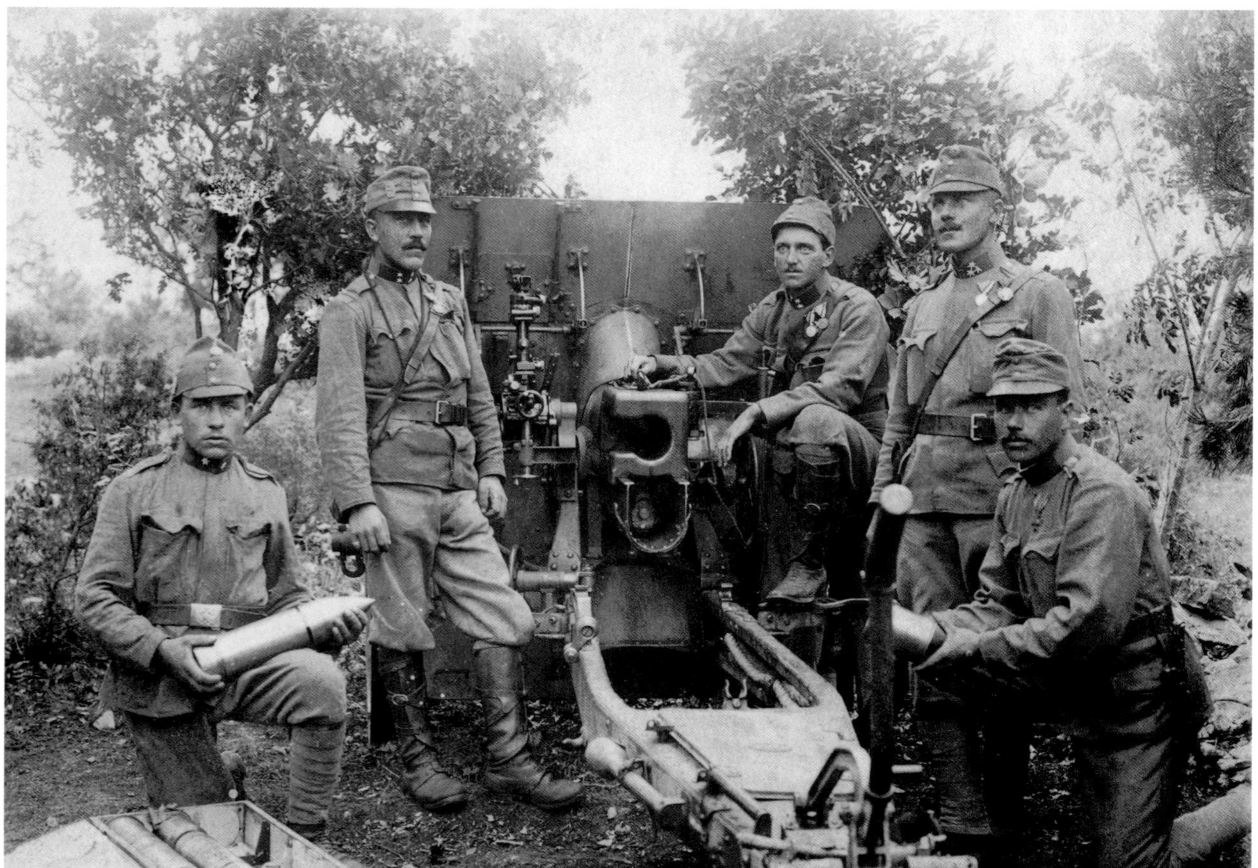

Five crew members pose for a photo of a breech view of a 10 cm *Feldhaubitz* M14 on the eastern front in 1915.

A 10cm *Feldhaubitz* with ammunition caisson M14 in a camouflaged position on the southern front in 1917.

A 30.5cm *Mörser* M11 on the southern front in 1916.

Left: A 30.5cm *Mörser* M11 on the eastern front in 1915. Below: Loading a 30.5cm *Mörser* M11 on the eastern front in 1915.

Loading a 30.5cm *Mörser* M11 on the southern front in 1917. The crew has dug in this *Mörser*.

A 30.5cm *Mörser* M11 on the southern front in 1917.

A 30.5cm *Mörser* M11 on the eastern front in 1915.

A breech view 30.5cm *Mörser* M11 on the eastern front in 1916.

A 30.5cm *Mörser* M11 on the southern front in 1917.

Inspecting a 30.5cm *Mörser* M11 on the eastern front in 1915.

Archduke (*Erzherzog*) Friedrich inspecting a 30.5cm *Mörser* M11 on the eastern front in 1915.

A unit poses with their *Mörser* on the southern front. From left to right; a 9cm M14 mortar; a *Scheinwerfer* or search light; a naval (*marine*) 4.7cm cannon which has been remounted; and a 6cm round small trench mortar.

This unit poses proudly with their pack horses, field telephones and the 3.5cm M15 cannon. Bruck an der Leithe 1916.

This unit poses with their field telephones, 3.5cm M15 cannons with wheel mounts, and open ammo boxes. Eastern front, 1916.

This *Korporal* poses next to his 3.5cm M15 cannon in a trench on the eastern front in 1916.

Transporting a *Minenwerfer* to the eastern front in 1915.

This crew poses with their field telephone and 8cm *Feldhaubitz* M 5/8 inside a sod-covered bunker on the eastern front in 1916.

This crew poses with their cannon on a cold winter day in Inzerdorf, Austria in 1917. The soldier wearing the goggles has won the silver bravery medal 1st class.

A very well camouflaged 8cm *Feldhaubitz* M 5/8 on the eastern front in 1915.

A pre to very early war photo of a crew and their 8cm *Feldhaubitz* M 5/8. The soldier standing in front of the cannon on the right wears an artillerist's cordage (*Vormeisterschnurr).*

This crew is trying to move their 8cm *Feldhaubitz* M 5/8 into position before an aerial attack. This photo was taken on the south western front in 1917.

The crew of *Batterie Nr. 2* poses next to their 8cm *Feldhaubitz* M 5/8 behind a camouflaged position on the snowy eastern front in 1915. The enlisted soldier on the left wears a white and red enamel *k.u.k U-Boot Kappe Abzeichen* which could be purchased to help support *Kriegs Waisen und Witwe* or War Orphans and Widows. The *k.u.k Kriegsmarine* was popular with all branches of the *k.u.k* armed forces.

This crew poses next to their 8cm *Feldhaubitz* M 5/8 and ammunition/repair tool caisson in a concealed position the eastern front in 1916.

An 8cm *Feldhaubitz* M 5/8 in a concealed position on the southern front in 1917.

This crew poses next to their camouflaged 8cm *Feldhaubitz* M 5/8 on the eastern front in 1915.

A breech view of an 8cm *Feldhaubitz* M 5/8 on the eastern front in 1915.

Soldiers transporting artillery on the southern front in 1917.

Gebirgsartillerietrain or mountain artillery transport in Carpathia in 1916.

Gebirgsartillerietrain or mountain artillery transport in Carpathia in 1916.

Transporting a heavy mortar (*Schwere Mörser*) on the eastern front in 1915.

A camouflaged 7.5cm *Feldhaubitz* M15 *Skodawerke A.G. Pilsen* on the eastern front in 1916.

Transporting 10cm M/14 cannons on the eastern front in 1916.

This crew poses with their modified 15cm M/80 on the eastern front in 1916.

This crew poses with their two 7cm M/14, a 10cm M/14 and observation equipment on the southern front in 1916.

This crew poses in front of their 9cm M75 (left) and a 12cm M80 on the southern front on January 13, 1917.

A munitions factory after an explosion in May 1918.

Transporting a 15cm long range *Geschütz* to the southern front in 1917.

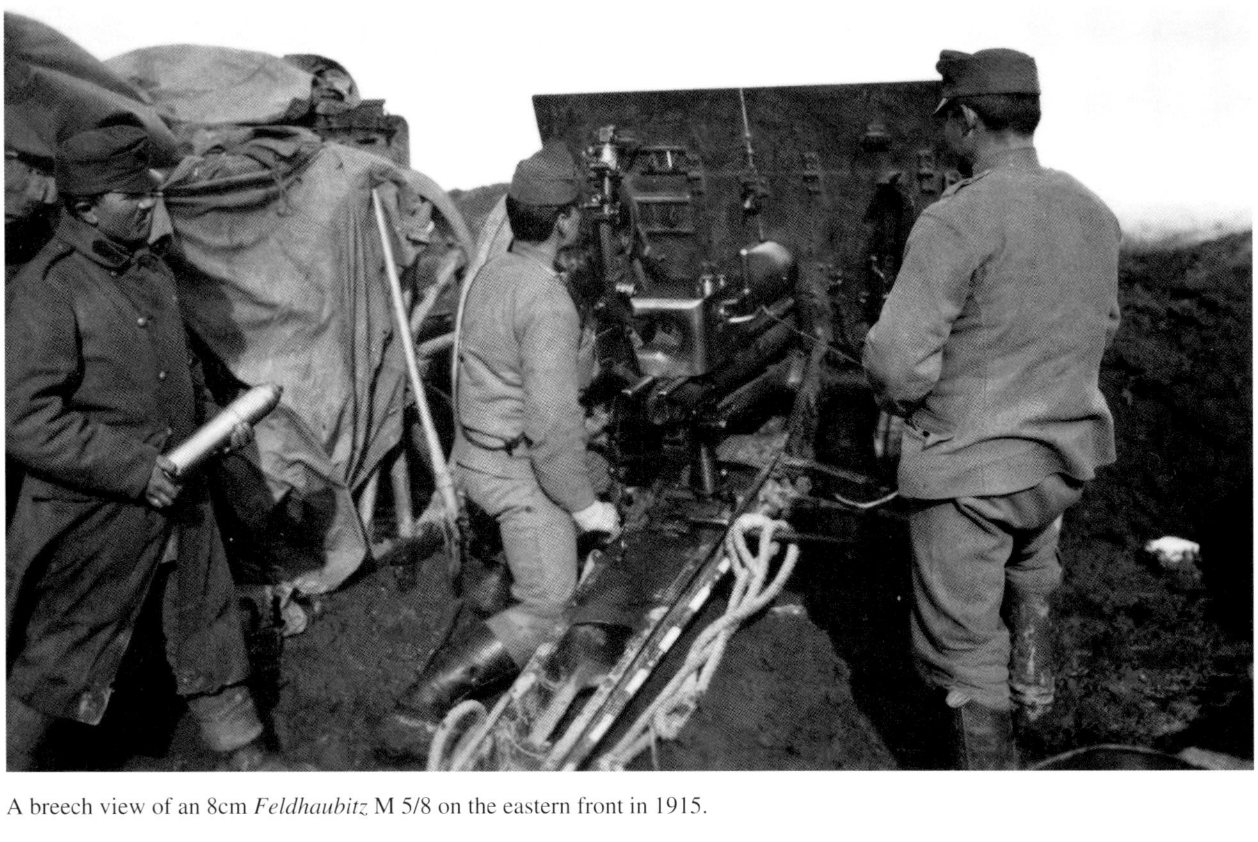

A breech view of an 8cm *Feldhaubitz* M 5/8 on the eastern front in 1915.

A destroyed 8cm *Feldhaubitz* M 5/8 on the eastern front in 1915.

This crew poses next to their 15cm M14/16 on southern front. March 9, 1916.

A staged photo during pre to very early war maneuvers. It appears as though those the bottles knocked out these soldiers before the bombardment did.

A 9cm M14 mortar in the trenches on the eastern front in 1916.

A *zugsfuehrer* and a *feldwebel* sending " *Pfingst Gruesse aus dem Felde. 1916*" or "Pentecost Greetings from the field. 1916." The *Feldwebel* sits on the munitions box for the 15cm M14 rounds displayed.

This crew is adjusting their 15cm M 94/4 on the eastern front in 1915.

Pre to early war photo of an artillery unit with 15cm M 94/4 cannons.

Heavy artillery in the Balkans.

This crew is preparing to load their 10cm M99 on the eastern front in 1915.

Two 15cm M99 cannons on a muddy road on the eastern front in 1915.

Heavy artillery on the eastern front in 1915.

A concealed heavy artillery emplacement on the eastern front in 1915.

A German officer observing an Austrian artillery crew load its heavy mortar (*Schwere Mörser*) on the southern front in 1917.

A heavy artillery piece in a forest on the eastern front in 1916.

A small trench mortar in a trench on the Isonzo front in 1917.

Heavy artillery unit on the eastern front in 1916.

A group photo of the *k.u.k Landwehr Feldkanonendivision Nr. 22* taken in Graz in 1915. Most of the soldiers wear the knitted wool, rolled stocking *Mütze* and early war gaiters or *Gamaschen.*

Early war photo of the *Ersatzkompanie Kader Nr. 1*. Most of the soldiers wear a pre to early war tunic and *feldmütze*.

This is a studio photo of an enlisted soldier wearing a summer weight tunic with painted field gray artillerist buttons.

This is a studio photo of a *Zugführer* in a *Karl's Bluse* with field gray celluloid artillerist buttons. Artillerists buttons were also made of carved bone (*Bein Knopf*) as well.

This *Leutnant* wears a private purchase pressed felt hat with gold thread stitched cockade and brass artillerist buttons. This photo was taken on the southern front in 1916.

An 8cm *Feldhaubitz* M 5/8 in a camouflaged position on the eastern front in 1916.

A studio photo of an *Unteroffizier* taken on June 20, 1918. He wears an *Ausgangskaeppi in schwarz* with brass artillerist buttons and a *feldgrau Mantel* with brass artillerist buttons.

A studio photo of a *Kanonier* or enlisted rank artillerist in an issue *feldgrau* uniform with brass artillerist buttons. He wears a Kaiser Karl cockade on his *feldmütze*.

A studio photo of an *Oberleutnant* taken in Trieste in 1917. He wears a private purchase pressed felt *feldmütze* with brass artillerist buttons and a fur lined tunic (Pelzrock) with brass artillerist buttons as well. On his *feldmütze* he wears the cap badge for the *Feld. Haubitz Regiment Nr. 28* and on his *Pelzrock,* the red and white enamel with green enamel wreath military service cross. The cavalry spurs on his boots indicate he may have been with a mounted artillery unit.

A studio photo of a *Kanonier* in a *feldgrau* tunic with celluloid artillerist buttons. 1917.

Chapter Twenty-One

The Kaisers

Kaiser Franz Joseph I

Kaiser Franz Joseph I on an official Jubilee Correspondence card. 1908 is also historically significant because on October 7, 1908 Austria annexed Bosnia and Herzegovina which infuriated Serbia and Montenegro who viewed this move to be deliberately detrimental in establishing a great South Slav state.

Kaiser Karl visiting the southern front in 1917

Kaiser Karl and Erzherzog Euegen visiting the southern front in 1917.

Kaiser Karl greetings troops before they leave for the southern front in 1917.

Aviators demonstrate a camera used for taking aerial photographs. 1917

Troops await Kaiser Karl while he visits with his generals and officers. 1917

Kaiser Karl greets highly decorated troops before they leave for the southern front in 1917

Vignettes

k.u.k Zugführer Karl Machherndl

Karl Machherndl was a Zugführer in the k.u.k Sappeur Baon 7/2. He saw action in Serbia, Russia and Tyrol. While in service he was awarded the Silver Bravery Medal first and second class, bronze bravery medal, six year service medal, 1908 military jubilee cross, the 1906 Pioneer badge and the Kaiser Karl Truppen Kreuz.

He was also attached a *Luftminenwerfer Baon* (Air powered trench mortars).

k.u.k Zugführer Karl Machherndl (left) wearing the Silver Bravery Medal first class, bronze bravery medal, and the Kaiser Karl Truppen Kreuz.

k.u.k Landesschützen Patrollienfuehrer Jakob Kollnig

Jakob Kollnig served in the 3 Schwadron der Reitenden-Tiroler-Landesschützen Division(3rd Squadron of the Mounted Tyrolean Landesschützen Division). He saw action in Poland, Russia and Tyrol. On 16th and 17th of September in 1916 he was awarded the Silver Bravery medal first class. The document papers for his silver bravery medal (Belohnungsantrag 609301) describe his actions as follows:

"In recognition of brave behavior before enemy forces on the night September 16th and 17th in 1916, he volunteered for a reconnaissance patrol (Spähtrupp) during an attack by a company of enemy soldiers. While under heavy enemy fire he traversed a treacherous minefield laid by his own soldiers to repel the advancing enemy.

Landesschütze Kollnig repeatedly displayed personal courage after this day and volunteered for more dangerous missions whereby he earned the respect and increased the moral of his fellow Kameraden.

He is a dashing and brave Patrollienführer and is indeed worthy of this decoration."

On November 15, 1917 he won the bronze bravery medal for taking part in distributing propaganda leaflets (Flugzettel) behind enemy lines.

On February 12, 1918 he was promoted to Landesschützen Patrollienführer and eight days later he was awarded the Kaiser Karl Truppen Kreuz.

Color Gallery

Patriotic postcards of Southern Front Battles

Above: This is a patriotic postcard which reads "Our heroes in a battle against the *Bersaglieri* . The *Bersaglieri* are an elite Italian fighting unit. Above Right: This is a patriotic postcard which reads "Fighting against the Italians. Repel of an Italian attack on the Isonzo front."

This is a patriotic postcard produced by the Red Cross to help support the war effort. The title reads "Defense of the High Mountains."

Right: This is a patriotic postcard produced by the Red Cross to help support the war effort. Depicted in this scene is an Austrian *Gebirgsjäger* ready to hurl a grenade down upon a group of *Alpini's*, The *Alpini's* are the Italian mountain troops.

Patriotic postcards of Machine Gunners

This is a patriotic postcard produced by the Red Cross to help the war effort. The title reads " Machinegun detachment"

Patriotic regimental postcards

This is an official "*Feldpostkarte*" or battlefield post from the *k.u.k Infantrie Regiment Freiherr von Bolfras Nr. 84.* These were sold to help the widows and orphans of the "84er" who died in battle.

The A.E.I.O.U. is an acronym for *Austria Est Imperatore Orbi Universum.* The patriotic poem at the bottoms of the card reads "Austria's Eagle climbs upward, sounding out with the call of the chorus: Our banners will wave victoriously and Austria will stand forever!" The double headed eagle or *Doppel Adler* was the symbol or crest of the empire and the monarchy. The double-headed eagle was a fitting choice because it looks to Austria's Empire in the east and in the west.

This is a regimental postcard from the *k.u.k Infantrie Regiment von Gaudernak Nr. 85.*

Patriotic postcards of the Austrians and Germans as brothers in arms (Waffenbrüder)

Sharing a common language, Austria allied itself with Germany and emphasized the need for a close togetherness as depicted in the patriotic postcard which reads " Brothers in arms for today and always thereafter". Not all Austrians felt this kinship nor did they feel that it was strategically the best move for Austria. The other option, was the strategy of a Threefold Monarchy (*Dreifaltige Monarchie*) which would have incorporated in addition to Hungary the other Slavic nations in the empire in similar alliance. This decision proved to be fatal to the monarchy. Before 1918, the Western power did want to see the monarchy break up but, when the German offensive in the west began in 1918, the allies found no other choice than to hasten the break up of the monarchy. Once the monarchy was broken up, the military collapsed and in October of 1918 the South Slavs, Czechs, and Poles seceded.

Wounded Austrian and German soldiers listen to this *Zugführer* tell, as the title indicates, his "War Adventures."

This is a patriotic postcard emphasizing the *Waffenbrüderschaft*. It reads " Hold out ! Hold out! Let the banners wave, showing the world how we loyally stand together!"

Erzherzog Karl, who would later become Kaiser Karl, visiting soldier on the Russian front in 1915.

Cap Badges (Kappe abzeichen)

Column 1
1.) *k.u.k Gesteinbohr Bataillon* - k.u.k rock drilling battalion
2.) *k.u.k Kraftfahrtruppe Turkei Weltkrieg* - k.u.k Motor Corps in Turkey (World War I)
3.) *Kampf Gruppe Landro 1916* - Combat Group Landro 1916
4.) *Weihnachten im Felde 1916* - k.u.k Feldtransportleitung No. 9 Christmas in the Battlefields 1916 k.u.k Battlefield Transport Control No. 9

Column 2
1) *Edelweiss 1914-1916* - Edelweiss 1914-1916 patriotic pin
2) *k.u.k Infantrie Regiment Schikofsy Nr. 83* - k.u.k Infantrie Regiment Schikofsy No. 83
3.) *1914-16 Eisenbahnsicherungs* - 1914-16 Railroad Guards
4.) *k.u.k Kurier-Posten des A.O.K.* k.u.k courier/messenger/mail troops

Column 3
1.) *4 Weihnachten in Felde 1917* - 4th Christmas in the field 1917
2.) *Brükenkopf Iwangorod 5. VIII . 1915* - Bridgehead Iwangorod August 5, 1915
3.) *Heeresgruppe Erherzog Eugen 1916* - Army Command/Group of Archduke Eugene 1916
4.) *Gruppe Luebke 1916-1917* - Luebke Squad/Group 1916-1917

Column 4
1.) *Honvéd Strum Bataillon 155* - Hungarian Assault troops battalion 155
2.) Offensiv gegen Italien - The Offensive against Italy
3.) *1914 30.5cm Mörser* - 1914 30.5cm Heavy Mortar
4.) *Weihnachten 1915* - Christmas 1915

Column 1
1.) *40 Honvéd Tábori Tarackos Ezred*
Hungarian Field Artillery Regiment No. 40
2.) *k.k. Kraft-Auto-Truppe im Weltkrieg 1914-16*
k.u.k Motor Corps in the World War 1914-16
3.) *k.u.k Feld Transportleitung X. 1914-16*
k.u.k Field Transport Control No. 10 1914-16
4.) *k.u.k Korps Hoffmann Mob. Res. Spital. 10/5*
k.u.k Corps Hoffmann Mobil Reserve Hospital 10/5

Column 2
1.) *Schützen Division Nr. 21*
Schützen Division No. 21
2.) *K.u.K Res. F. K. R. No. 73*
K.u.K Reserve Field Canon Regiment No. 73
3.) *Kaiser Franz Joseph I 1830-1916*
Kaiser Franz Joseph I praying 1830-1916
4.) *Den Kreigern Steirmarks 1914-15*
The Warrior Styrians 1914-15

Column 3
1.) *Sanitats Abteilung 1914-1916*
Medical Unit 1914-1916
2.) *Heil 1915! Gott straff die Englander!*
Hail 1915! God punish the British!
3.) *K.M.G.A. (Kavalrie Maschinen Gewehr Abteilung)*
Cavalry Machinegun Unit
4.) *k.k. Landst. Inf. Baon Nr. 75*
k.u.k Landsturm Infantry Battalion No. 75

Column 4
1.) *Telefon/Telegragh kappenabzeichen*
Telephone/Telegraph cap badge.
2.) *Österreiches Rotes Kreuz*
Austrian Red Cross
3.) *Kreigshilfedeinst. Wiener Freiwillige Rettungsgesellschaft. IX. Dec. 1881. 1914.*
War help service. Viennese volunteers rescue society founded December 9 1881. 1914.

Front and Reverse views of *Left*: Privately commissioned and purchased enamel on bronze pilot's breast badge. (Feldpilotabzeichen.) and *Right*: A well worn enamel on bronze pilot's breast badge. (Feldpilotabzeichen.) Two crowns represent the Austria (right with missing cross) and Hungary (left with the Crown of St. Stephan. The body of the eagle has a concave casting and does not bear it's manufacturer's name, Zimbler.

Front and Reverse views of *Left*: General Airmen's Badge (*Allgemeines Fliegerabzeichen)* silver and enamel in miniature. Silver hallmark is on the right tip of the eagle's wing. "K" stands for Kaiser Karl.*Right*: Silver enameled Zimbler "FJI." flight badge (*Feldpilotabzeichen*) miniature. Seen on the needle are silver hallmarks. Engraving reads " *5 X. 1916— Erinnerung an Feggo*" (October 5th, 1916 —In memory of Feggo).

Front and Reverse views of *Left*: Enamel on gilded bronze Allgemeine Fliegerabzeichen in miniature. The "K" is for Kaiser Karl. *Right*: Enamel on bronze *Feldpilotabzeichen* in miniature. Unusual is the "K" for Kaiser Karl with one crown. Normally there would appear two crowns.

Two assault troop rings. The ring on the left is silver and is hallmarked, while the ring on the right is gilded.

See captions opposite page.

Issue *Hechtgrau Feldmütze. Montur Depot* stamped 1911 (MD 1911).

Collar Insignia (top to bottom, left column to far right)
1) *Maschinengewehr Kragenabzeichen für Offiziere* - Machinegunner collar insignia for officers
2)*Maschinengewehr Kragenabzeichen für Unteroffiziere* - Machinegunner collar insignia for non commissioned officers
3)*Maschinengewehr Kragenabzeichen für Mannschaft* - Machinegunner collar insignia for enlisted soldiers
4) *Honved ge'puska'sok/* Ungarisch maschinengewehr - Hungarian Machine gunner collar insignia. (Note: The crown of St. Stephen with tilted cross)
5) *Allgemeine Maschinengewehr abzeichen* - General Machinegunner insignia.
6) *Telefon/Telegraf Kragenabzeichen für Offiziere* Telephone/Telegraph operator collar insignia for officers
7) *Telefon/Telegraf Kragenabzeichen für Unteroffiziere* Telephone/Telegraph operator collar insignia for noncommissioned officers
8) *Emailliert/Gemahlt Telefon/Telegraf Kragenabzeichen für Offiziere/Unteroffiziere* - Enameled/Painted Telephone/Telegraph operator collar insignia for officers and NCOs
9) *Telefon/Telegraf Kragenabzeichen für Mannschaft* Telephone/Telegraph operator collar insignia for enlisted soldiers
10) *Stoff Telefon/Telegraf Kragenabzeichen für Offiziere/Unteroffiziere* - Gold thread on cloth Telephone/Telegraph operator collar insignia for officers and NCOs
11) *Minenwerfer/ Granatenwerfer Kragenabzeichen für Offiziere* - Trench mortar collar insignia for officers
12) *Minenwerfer/ Granatenwerfer Kragenabzeichen für Unteroffiziere* - Trench mortar collar insignia for non commissioned officers
13) *Scheinwerfer Kragenabzeichen* - Spot light collar insignia
14) *Kraftfahrer Kragenabzeichen* - Motor Corps collar insignia
15) *Pionier Kragenabzeichen* - Pioneer/Engineer collar insignia
16) *Flieger/Ballonisten Kragenabzeichen* - Aviator/ balloonist collar insignia
17) *Eisenbahn Kragenabzeichen* - Railroad collar insignia
18) *Elektriker für Eisenbahn und Kraftfahrzeug Kragenabzeichen für Offiziere* - Electricians attached to railway and motor corps units collar insignia for officers
19) *Elektriker für Eisenbahn und Kraftfahrzeug Kragenabzeichen für Unteroffiziere* - Electricians attached to railway and motor corps units collar insignia for non commissioned officers
20) *Edelweiss Kragenabzeichen* - Edelweiss collar insignia

Pre to early war private purchase *Hechtgrau Schiffchen*.

Private purchase crushable pressed felt *feldgrau Feldmütze*. Blue felt cross is a unit identification marking possibly for the Hoch und Deutschmeister Regiment Nr. 4.

Private purchase feldgrau *Schiffchen*. The red "3K" is a unit identification marking.

Hechtgrau field kepi (*Feldkäppi*).

Ausgangskäppi in schwarz Black dress/walking out kepi from 24 Jaeger battalion.

Summer weight flight cap which was later winterized.

Above and Opposite: Aviator flight gloves (*Flieger Handschue*) made of deer leather (*Hirschleder*) and rabbit fur (*Hasepelz*).

Folding glass flight goggles.

Issued shoes (*Schue)* and leather gaiters (*Ledergamaschen*) . The shoes are stamped with the size 42 and the date "16" 1916. The wood pegs seen around the outside of the sole helped hold the shoe together under wet conditions, because as the wood pegs absorbed water they expanded. Ledergamaschen are Montur Depot dated 1916 (MD 1916).

Identified aviator's medal grouping. Grouping includes an FJI. Zimbler Aviator breast badge in original box , two Zimbler miniature flight badges, a German Aviator Badge in miniature, a Gut Land depicting St. Elias badge, and a Kaiser Wilhelm and Kaiser Franz Joseph I patriotic pin. The red felt glued on back of the breast badge kept the badge from rubbing against the tunic. Both miniatures are manufactured by Zimbler however each is slightly different. Both have different needles, one has blue enamel ribbons, and the other has the more commonly seen red ribbons.

Dragonerhelm für Mannschaft Model 1850. Dragoon helmet for enlisted men. Model 1850. Leather and metal construction.

Dragonerhelm fuer unteroffizier Model 1850. Dragoon helmet for Non-commissioned officers. Model 1850. Leather and metal construction.

Dragonerhelm für Fähnrich. Model 1850. Dragoon helmet for Cadets Model 1850. Metal construction.

Dragonerhelm für Officiate mit Kasten/Behälter. Dragoon officer helmet Model 1850 with case. Metal construction (Helmet). Leather, wood and cloth construction (Case).

WWI Austrian manufactured aluminum M16 Stahlhelm. Later repainted in the 1930's .

Snow goggles (*Schneebrille*).

Glacier goggles (*Gletscherbrille*).

Gas mask goggles for horses. Celluloid lenses with leather cushioned backing.

Artillery sight manufactured by Otto Ganser in Vienna. This sight was mounted on the 9cm M75/96 field canon and also could be modified to fit on other field canons as well.

Artillery Gauge for the 10cm Feld Haubitz M.14 manufactured by Otto Ganser in Vienna.

Neubronner's Doppel-Sport Brieftauben-Kamera: First aerial panoramic camera for use with carrier pidgeons during WWI. This is an original, which is extremely rare, and includes the patent and literature. 1908.

Reflex 755, 9 x 12cm. 1915.

Zeiss Ballon Kamera: Unknown aerial camera for use from balloons. Includes a built-in watch and altimeter. Data was recorded by the stereo lenses and shutter inside the camera. Delivered to St. Petersburg 1911.

Glossary

Austrian/German

A. E. I. O.U. - Austria Est Imperare Orbi Universo
Abwehr - to block, defend, repulse
Abteilung - detachment/ squad/ division
Abzeichen - insignia/marking/badge
Allgemeines - general/compulsory
Ausgang - going out/walking out/dress
Baon - battalion
Beilpicke- pick-axe
Bekleidungs Amt- clothing department/ agency. B. A. with a date was stamped on all issued clothing
Beobachter - observer/onlooker/ spotter
Berndorf(er) - Austrian Metal Producer. During the war this firm produced helmets referred to as "Berndorfers". The Berndorfer is easily recognized by its distinctive shape(s), the circular metal disk ventilation guard on top and by the firm's logo (Berndorfer bear) which is stamped inside the back part of the helmet.
Bluse- field tunic
Brandpfeile – literal translation "burning or flaming arrows". These were incendiary devices in a projectile form, which were thrown from aircraft.
Doppel Adler- The double-headed eagle which was the symbol and crest of the empire and monarchy. This crest appeared on pre to early war helmets and shakos, and later occasionally on an officer's or guards Berndorfer. Bayonets and guns were also stamped with this crest. The Doppel Adler was used during the interwar years as well however instead of the eagle heads having crowns they had halos or heiligenschein.
Dolch- dagger/knife
Einheit- unit
Eisenbahn - railroad
Feldbluse- field tunic
Feldgrau - field gray
Feldflasche- canteen
Feldhaubitz- field cannon/ howitzer
Feldkanon - field cannon
Feldkappe- field cap
Feldküche - field kitchen
Feldmütze - field cap
Feldpilot- field/combat pilot
Feldspital- field hospital
Feldwebel - sergeant
Flieger- pilot/aviator
Fliegerabzeichen- pilot's badge
Fliegerbrille - pilot's goggles
Fliegerpfeile – literal translation "aviator's arrows" Aviation fleschettes or iron darts.
Fliegerkorps - Air corps
Gasmaske- gasmask
Gefreiter - lance corporal/private first class
Gendarme (rie) - military police
Gamaschen- leggings/puttees
Geschütz - Heavy artillery/guns
Gewehr - gun/rifle
Graben - ditch, trench, moat
Granatenwerfer - grenade thrower/ mortar
Handmaschinengewehr- hand / mobile machine gun unit
Handschue- gloves
Haubitz - Artillery piece/ cannon/ howitzer
Hauptmann- captain
Hechtgrau - Pike (fish gray/sea gray/blue gray)
Jäger - hunter
Kader- cadre
Käppi / Kaeppi - kepi
kaiserlich und königlich (k.u.k) - imperial and royal
Kaiser Jäger - Emperor's hunter
Kaiser's Schützen - Emperor's guard
Kalbsfelltornister- calfskin covered backpack
Kappeabzeichen- cap badges
Kolonne- column
Kraftfahrer - driver/motorist
Kragenabzeichen- collar insignia
Kreuz- cross
Kriegsmetall- wartime composite metal
Landwehr- reserve troops
Lazarett- military hospital
Ledergamaschen- leather gaitors/leggings
Leuchsatz - light emitting matter
Luftfahrerabzeichen – Airman's Badge
Mannschaft - enlisted rank
Mantel- overcoat
Maschinengewehr- machine gun
Minenwerfer - trench mortar
Montur - outfit/ get up
Montur Depot- outfitting depot M.D. with a date was stamped on all issue clothing and equipment.
Mörser - large mortar
Österreich- German for Austria. Literal translation means Empire of the East or Eastern Kingdom.
Oberst- colonel

Pantalons- pants
Panzerzug- armored train
Pelzrock- fur lined tunic
Rock- tunic
Riemen-straps/ sling
Schiffchen - forage cap or a field cap without a visor
Schwarzlose- Austrian machinegun manufacturer.
Standschützen - Militia. This term is associated Tyrolean soldiers.
steigeisen- iron cleats
Steingrau - stone grey
Stutzen- short rifle
Truppen - Troops/ unit
Unteroffizier- NCO / non commissioned officer
Vormeisterschnurr- artillerist cordage
Vorschriften- regulations manual
Wachzimmer- guardroom
Zugführer- platoon leader
Zug- column/ platoon/squad

Hungarian/ Magyar

csakany- pick axe
cspat- troops
csukaszürkében- pike blue/ blue gray- hechtgrau
ezred- regiment
gazalarcban- gasmask
géppuskások- machinegun
gylalog-erzed- infantry regiment
Hadnagy- Leutnant
Honvéd- Hungarian armed forces
huszárok- hussars. Literal translation means "free boot"
kiralyi - royal
Levetett hátborönd- calfskin covered backpack
lovasság - cavalry
loveszarok- trench
Magyarnadrág- Hungarian/Honvéd pants.
Õrmester- sergeant
Õrnagy- major
Õrvezetõ- private
puska- rifle
roham zaszloalj- assault battalion
százados- captain
szakaszvezetõ- platoon leader
szakasz- platoon
Táboriszuerkében- field gray
Tábori sapka- field cap
Tiszti- officer
Tüzérség- artillery
Vilag haboru - world war
Zubbony- tunic

Appendix

k.u.k Infantry Regiments

1. *k.u.k. Infantrie Regiment Kaiser Nr. 1* (k.u.k Infantry Regiment Kaiser No. 1)

2. *k.u.k Infantrie Regiment Alexander I. Kaiser von Russland Nr. 2* (k.u.k Infantry Regiment Alexander I Emperor of Russia)

3. *k.u.k Infantrie Regiment Erzherzog Karl Nr. 3* (k.u.k Infantry Regiment Archduke Charles No. 3)

4. *k.u.k. Infantrie Regiment Hoch und Deutschmeister Nr. 4* (k.u.k. Infantry Regiment of the high Teutonic Order No.. 4)

5. *k.u.k. Infantrie Regiment Freiherr von Klobucar Nr. 5* (k.u.k. Infantry Regiment Baron von Klobucar No. 5)

6. *k.u.k. Infantrie Regiment Karl I Koenig von Ruemanien Nr. 6* (k.u.k. Infantry Regiment Charles I, King of Rumania)

7. *k.u.k. Infantrie Regiment Graf von Khevenhueller Nr. 7* (k.u.k. Infantry Regiment Count von Khevenhueller No. 7)

8. *k.u.k. Infantrie Regiment Erzherzog Karl Stephan Nr. 8* (k.u.k. Infantry Regiment Archduke Charles Stephan No. 8)

9. *k.u.k. Infantrie Regiment Graf Clerfayt Nr. 9* (k.u.k. Infantry Regiment Count Clerfayt No. 9)

10. *k.u.k. Infantrie Regiment Gustav V. von Schweden, der Gotten und Wenden Nr. 10* (k.u.k. Infantry Regiment Gustav V. of Sweden, Gods of the Heavens)

11. *k.u.k. Infantrie Regiment Johann Georg Prinz von Sachsen Nr. 10* (k.u.k. Infantry Regiment Johann George, Prince of Saxony)

12. *k.u.k. Infantrie Regiment Parmann Nr. 12* (k.u.k. Infantry Regiment Parmann No. 12)

13. *k.u.k. Infantrie Regiment Jung-Starhemberg Nr. 13* (k.u.k. Infantry Regiment Young/New-Starhemberg No. 13)

14. *k.u.k. Infantrie Regiment Ernst Ludwig Grossherzog von Hessen und bei Rhein Nr. 14* (k.u.k. Infantry Regiment Ernst Ludwig Grandduke of Hessen and on the Rhine No. 14)

15. *k.u.k. Infantrie Regiment Freiherr von Georgi Nr. 15* (k.u.k. Infantry Regiment Baron of George No. 15)

16. *k.u.k. Infantrie Regiment Freiherr von Giesl Nr. 16* (k.u.k. Infantry Regiment Baron of Giesl No. 16)

17. *k.u.k. Infantrie Regiment Ritter von Milde Nr. 17* (k.u.k. Infantry Regiment Knight of Milde No. 17)

18. *k.u.k. Infantrie Regiment Erzherzog Leopold Salvator Nr. 18* (k.u.k. Infantry Regiment Archduke Leopold Salvator No. 18)

19. *k.u.k. Infantrie Regiment Erzherzog Franz Ferdinand Nr. 19* (k.u.k. Infantry Regiment Archduke Franz Ferdinand No. 19)

20. *k.u.k. Infantrie Regiment Heinrich Prinz von Preussen Nr. 20* (k.u.k. Infantry Regiment Heinrich Prince of Prussia No. 20)

21. *k.u.k. Infantrie Regiment Graf von Abensperg und Traun Nr. 21* (k.u.k. Infantry Regiment Count of Abensperg and Traun No. 21

22. *k.u.k. Infantrie Regiment Graf von Lacy Nr. 22* (k.u.k. Infantry Regiment Count of Lacy No. 22)

23. *k.u.k. Infantrie Regiment von Baden Nr. 23* (k.u.k. Infantry Regiment of Baden No. 23)

24. *k.u.k. Infantrie Regiment Ritter von Kummer Nr. 24* (k.u.k. Infantry Regiment Knight of Kummer No. 24)

25. *k.u.k. Infantrie Regiment von Pokorny Nr. 25* (k.u.k. Infantry Regiment of Pokorny No. 25)

26. *k.u.k. Infantrie Regiment Schreiber Nr. 26* (k.u.k. Infantry Regiment Schreiber No. 26)

27. *k.u.k. Infantrie Regiment Albert I. Koenig der Belgier Nr. 27* (k.u.k. Infantry Regiment Albert I. King of Belgium No. 27)

28. *k.u.k. Infantrie Regiment Viktor Emanuel III. Koenig von Italien Nr. 28* (k.u.k. Infantry Regiment Victor Emanuel III, King of Italy No. 28)

29. *k.u.k. Infantrie Regiment Freiherr von Loudon Nr. 29* (k.u.k. Infantry Regiment Baron of Loudon No. 29)

30. *k.u.k. Infantrie Regiment Schoedler Nr. 30* (k.u.k. Infantry Regiment Schoedler No. 30)

31. *k.u.k. Infantrie Regiment Pucherna Nr. 31* (k.u.k. Infantry Regiment Pucherna No. 31)

32. *k.u.k. Infantrie Regiment Kaiserin und Koenigin Maria Theresia Nr. 32* (k.u.k. Infantry Regiment Empress and Queen Maria Theresa No. 32)

33. *k.u.k. Infantrie Regiment Kaiser Leopold II Nr. 33* (k.u.k. Infantry Regiment Kaiser Leopold II, No. 33)

34. *k.u.k. Infantrie Regiment Wilhelm I. Deutscher Kaiser und Koenig von Preußen Nr. 34* (k.u.k Infantry Regiment Wilhelm I. German Emperor and King of Prussia No. 34

35. *k.u.k Infantrie Regiment Freiherr von Sterneck Nr. 35* (k.u.k Infantry Regiment Baron of Sterneck No. 35)

36. *k.u.k Infantrie Regiment Browne Nr. 36* (k.u.k Infantry Regiment Browne No. 36)

37. *k.u.k Infantrie Regiment Erzherzog Joseph Nr. 37*(k.u.k Infantry Regiment Archduke Joseph No. 37)

38. *k.u.k Infantrie Regiment Alfons XIII. Koenig von Spanien Nr. 38* (k.u.k Infantry Regiment Alfonso King of Spain No. 38)

39. *k.u.k Infantrie Regiment Freiherr von Konrad Nr. 39* (k.u.k Infantry Regiment Baron of Conrad No. 39)

40. *k.u.k Infantrie Regiment Ritter von Pino Nr. 40* (k.u.k Infantry Regiment Knight of Pino No. 40)

41. *k.u.k. Infantrie Regiment Erzherzog Eugen Nr. 41* (k.u.k. Infantry Regiment Archduke Eugene Nr. 41)

42. *k.u.k. Infantrie Regiment Ernst August Herzog von Cumberland, Herzog zu Braunschweig und Lueneburg Nr. 42* (k.u.k. Infantry Regiment Ernst August Duke of Cumberland, Duke of Braunschweig and Lueneburg No. 42)

43. *k.u.k Infantrie Regiment Rupprecht Kronprinz von Bayern Nr. 43* (k.u.k. Infantry Regiment Crown Prince of Bavaria No. 43)

44. *k.u.k. Infantrie Regiment Erzherzog Albrecht Nr. 44* (k.u.k. Infantry Regiment Archduke Albrecht No. 44)

45. *k.u.k Infantrie Regiment Erzherzog Joseph Ferdinand Nr. 45 (*k.u.k. Infantry Regiment Archduke Joseph Ferdinand No. 45)

46. *k.u.k Infantrie Regiment Freiherr von Fejervary Nr. 46 (*k.u.k. Infantry Regiment Baron of Fejervary No. 46)

47. *k.u.k. Infantrie Regiment Graf von Beck-Rzikowsky Nr. 47* (k.u.k. Infantry Regiment Count of Beck-Rzikowsky No. 47)

48. *k.u.k. Infantrie Regiment Rohr Nr. 48* (k.u.k. Infantry Regiment Rohr No. 48)

49. *k.u.k. Infantrie Regiment Freiherr von Hess Nr. 49* (k.u.k. Infantry Regiment Count of Hess Nr. 49)

50. *k.u.k. Infantrie Regiment Friedrich Grossherzog von Baden Nr. 50* (k.u.k. Infantry Regiment Grand Duke of Baden No. 50)

51. *k.u.k. Infantrie Regiment von Boroevic Nr. 51* (k.u.k. Infantry Regiment of Boroevic No. 51)

52. *k.u.k. Infantrie Regiment Erzherzog Friedrich Nr. 52* (k.u.k. Infantry Regiment Archduke Erzherzog Friedrich No. 52)

53. *k.u.k. Infantrie Regiment Dankl Nr. 53* (k.u.k. Infantry Regiment Dankl No. 53)

54. *k.u.k. Infantrie Regiment Alt-Starhemberg Nr. 54* (k.u.k. Infantry Regiment Old-Starhemberg No. 54)

55. *k.u.k. Infantrie Regiment Nikolaus I. Koenig von Montenegro Nr. 55* (k.u.k. Infantry Regiment Nicholas I. King of Montenegro No. 55)

56. *k.u.k. Infantrie Regiment Graf Daun Nr. 56* (k.u.k. Infantry Regiment Count Daun No. 56)

57. *k.u.k. Infantrie Regiment Prinz zu Sachsen-Koburg-Saalfeld Nr. 57* (k.u.k. Infantry Regiment Prince of Saxony-Coburg-Saalfeld No. 57)

58. *k.u.k. Infantrie Regiment Erzherzog Ludwig Salvator Nr. 58* (k.u.k. Infantry Regiment Archduke Ludwig Salvator No. 58)

59. *k.u.k. Infantrie Regiment Erzherzog Rainer Nr. 59* (k.u.k. Infantry Regiment Archduke Rainer No. 59)

60. *k.u.k. Infantrie Regiment Ritter von Ziegler Nr. 60* (k.u.k. Infantry Regiment Knight of Ziegler No. 60)

61. *k.u.k. Infantrie Regiment Ritter von Frank Nr. 61* (k.u.k. Infantry Regiment Knight of Frank No. 61)

62. *k.u.k. Infantrie Regiment Ludwig III.* (k.u.k. Infantry Regiment Ludwig III.

63. *k.u.k. Infantrie Regiment Freiherr von Pitreich Nr. 63* (k.u.k. Infantry Regiment Baron of Pitreich No. 63)

64. *k.u.k. Infantrie Regiment Ritter von Auffenberg Nr. 64* (k.u.k. Infantry Regiment Knight of Auffenberg No. 64)

65. *k.u.k. Infantrie Regiment Erzherzog Ludwig Viktor Nr. 65* (k.u.k. Infantry Regiment Archduke Ludwig Victor No. 65)

66. *k.u.k. Infantrie Regiment Erzherzog Peter Ferdinand Nr. 66* (k.u.k. Infantry Regiment Archduke Peter Ferdinand No. 66)

67. *k.u.k. Infantrie Regiment Freiherr Kray Nr. 67* (k.u.k. Infantry Regiment Baron Kray No. 67)

68. *k.u.k. Infantrie Regiment Freiherr von Reicher Nr. 68* (k.u.k. Infantry Regiment Baron of Reicher No. 68)

69. *k.u.k. Infantrie Regiment Freiherr von Leithner Nr. 69* (k.u.k. Infantry Regiment Baron of Leithner No. 69)

70. *k.u.k. Infantrie Regiment von Appel Nr. 70* (k.u.k. Infantry Regiment of Appel No. 70)

71. *k.u.k. Infantrie Regiment Galgotzy Nr. 71* (k.u.k. Infantry Regiment Galgotzy No. 71)

72. *k.u.k. Infantrie Regiment Freiherr von David* (k.u.k. Infantry Regiment Baron of David No. 72)

73. *k.u.k. Infantrie Regiment Albrecht Herzog von Wuerttemberg Nr. 73* (k.u.k. Infantry Regiment Albrecht Duke of Wuerttemberg No. 73)

74. *k.u.k. Infantrie Regiment Freiherr von Schoenaich Nr. 74* (k.u.k. Infantry Regiment Baron of Schoenaich No. 74)

75. *k.u.k. Infantrie Regiment Nr. 75* (k.u.k. Infantry Regiment No. 75)

76. *k.u.k. Infantrie Regiment Freiherr von Salis-Soglio Nr. 76* (k.u.k. Infantry Regiment Baron of Salis-Soglio No. 76)

77. *k.u.k. Infantrie Regiment Philip Herzog von Würtemberg Nr. 77* (k.u.k. Infantry Regiment Philip Duke of Würtemberg No. 77)

78. *k.u.k. Infantrie Regiment Gerba Nr. 78* (k.u.k. Infantry Regiment Gerba No. 78)

79. *k.u.k. Infantrie Regiment Graf Jellacic Nr. 79* (k.u.k. Infantry Regiment Count Graf Jellacic No. 79)

80. *k.u.k. Infantrie Regiment Wilhelm Ernst Grossherzog von Sachsen-Weimar-Eisenach, Herzog zu Sachsen Nr. 80* (k.u.k. Infantry Regiment Wilhelm Ernst Grand Duke of Saxony-Weimar-Eisenach, Duke to Saxony No. 80)

81. *k.u.k. Infantrie Regiment Freiherr Johann von Waldstaetten Nr. 81* (k.u.k. Infantry Regiment Baron John of Waldstaetten No. 81)

82. *k.u.k. Infantrie Regiment Freiherr von Schwitzer Nr. 82* (k.u.k. Infantry Regiment Baron of Schwitzer No. 82)

83. *k.u.k. Infantrie Regiment Schikofsky Nr. 83* (k.u.k. Infantry Regiment Schikofsky No. 83)

84. *k.u.k. Infantrie Regiment Freiherr von Bolfras Nr. 84* (k.u.k. Infantry Regiment Baron of Bolfras No. 84)

85. *k.u.k. Infantrie Regiment von Gaudernak Nr. 85* (k.u.k. Infantry Regiment of Gaudernak No. 85)

86. *k.u.k. Infantrie Regiment Freiherr von Steininger Nr. 86* (k.u.k. Infantry Regiment Baron of Steininger No. 86)

87. *k.u.k. Infantrie Regiment Freiherr von Succovaty Nr. 87* (k.u.k. Infantry Regiment Baron of Succovaty No. 87)

88. *k.u.k. Infantrie Regiment Nr. 88* (k.u.k. Infantry Regiment No. 88)

89. *k.u.k. Infantrie Regiment Freiherr von Albori Nr. 89* (k.u.k. Infantry Regiment Baron of Albori No. 89)

90. *k.u.k. Infantrie Regiment von Horsetzky Nr. 90* (k.u.k. Infantry Regiment of Horsetzky No. 90)

91. *k.u.k. Infantrie Regiment Freiherr von Czibulka Nr. 91* (k.u.k. Infantry Regiment Baron of Czibulka No. 91)

92. *k.u.k. Infantrie Regiment von Horstein Nr. 92* (k.u.k. Infantry Regiment of Horstein No. 92)

93. *k.u.k. Infantrie Regiment Nr. 93* (k.u.k. Infantry Regiment No. 93)

94. *k.u.k. Infantrie Regiment Freiherr von Koller Nr. 94* (k.u.k. Infantry Regiment Baron of Koller No. 94)

95. *k.u.k. Infantrie Regiment von Koevess Nr. 95* (k.u.k. Infantry Regiment of Koevess No. 95)

96. *k.u.k. Infantrie Regiment Ferdinand Kronprinz von Rumaenien Nr. 96* (k.u.k. Infantry Regiment Ferdinand Crown Prince of Rumania No. 96)

97. *k.u.k. Infantrie Regiment Freiherr Georg von Waldstaetten Nr. 97* (k.u.k. Infantry Regiment Baron George of Waldstaetten Nr. 97)

98 *k.u.k. Infantrie Regiment von Rummer Nr. 98* (k.u.k. Infantry Regiment of Rummer No. 98)

99. *k.u.k. Infantrie Regiment Nr. 99* (k.u.k. Infantry Regiment No. 99)

100. *k.u.k. Infantrie Regiment von Steinsberg Nr. 100* (k.u.k. Infantry Regiment of Steinsberg No. 100)

101. *k.u.k. Infantrie Regiment Freiherr von Drathschmidt Nr. 101* (k.u.k. Infantry Regiment Baron of Drathschmidt No. 101)

102. *k.u.k. Infantrie Regiment Potiorek Nr. 102* (k.u.k. Infantry Regiment Potiorek No. 102)

Kaiser Jaeger Regiments (Tyrolean)

1. *k.u.k. Regiment der Tiroler Kaiser Jaeger Nr. 1* (k.u.k. Regiment of the Tyrolean Kaiser Jaeger No. 1

2. *k.u.k. Regiment der Tiroler Kaiser Jaeger Nr. 2* (k.u.k. Regiment of the Tyrolean Kaiser Jaeger No. 2

3. *k.u.k. Regiment der Tiroler Kaiser Jaeger Nr. 3* (k.u.k. Regiment of the Tyrolean Kaiser Jaeger No. 3

4. *k.u.k. Regiment der Tiroler Kaiser Jaeger Nr. 4* (k.u.k. Regiment of the Tyrolean Kaiser Jaeger No. 4

Feld Jaeger Battalion

1. *k.u.k. Feld Jaeger bataillon Nr. 1* (k.u.k. Field Jaeger Battalion Nr. 1)

2. *k.u.k. Feld Jaeger bataillon Nr. 2* (k.u.k. Field Jaeger Battalion Nr. 2)

3. k.u.k. Feld Jaeger bataillon Nr. 3 (k.u.k. Field Jaeger Battalion Nr. 3)

4. k.u.k. Feld Jaeger bataillon Nr. 4 (k.u.k. Field Jaeger Battalion Nr. 4)

5. *k.u.k. Feld Jaeger bataillon Nr. 5* (k.u.k. Field Jaeger Battalion Nr. 5)

6. *k.u.k. Feld Jaeger bataillon Nr. 6* (k.u.k. Field Jaeger Battalion Nr. 6)

7. *k.u.k. Feld Jaeger bataillon Nr. 7* (k.u.k. Field Jaeger Battalion Nr. 7)

8. *k.u.k. Feld Jaeger bataillon Nr. 8* (k.u.k. Field Jaeger Battalion Nr. 8)

9. *k.u.k. Feld Jaeger bataillon Nr. 9* (k.u.k. Field Jaeger Battalion Nr. 9)

10. *k.u.k. Feld Jaeger bataillon Nr. 10* (k.u.k. Field Jaeger Battalion Nr. 10)

11. *k.u.k. Feld Jaeger bataillon Nr. 11* (k.u.k. Field Jaeger Battalion Nr. 11)

12. *k.u.k. Feld Jaeger bataillon Nr. 12* (k.u.k. Field Jaeger Battalion Nr. 12)

13. *k.u.k. Feld Jaeger bataillon Nr. 13* (k.u.k. Field Jaeger Battalion Nr. 13)

14. *k.u.k. Feld Jaeger bataillon Nr. 14* (k.u.k. Field Jaeger Battalion Nr. 14)

15. *k.u.k. Feld Jaeger bataillon Nr. 15* (k.u.k. Field Jaeger Battalion Nr. 15)

16. *k.u.k. Feld Jaeger bataillon Nr. 16* (k.u.k. Field Jaeger Battalion Nr. 16)

17. *k.u.k. Feld Jaeger bataillon Nr. 17* (k.u.k. Field Jaeger Battalion Nr. 17)

18. *k.u.k. Feld Jaeger bataillon Nr. 18* (k.u.k. Field Jaeger Battalion Nr. 18)

19. *k.u.k. Feld Jaeger bataillon Nr. 19* (k.u.k. Field Jaeger Battalion Nr. 19)

20. *k.u.k. Feld Jaeger bataillon Nr. 20* (k.u.k. Field Jaeger Battalion Nr. 20)

21. *k.u.k. Feld Jaeger bataillon Nr. 21* (k.u.k. Field Jaeger Battalion Nr. 21)

22. *k.u.k. Feld Jaeger bataillon Nr. 22* (k.u.k. Field Jaeger Battalion Nr. 22)

23. *k.u.k. Feld Jaeger bataillon Nr. 23* (k.u.k. Field Jaeger Battalion Nr. 23)

24. *k.u.k. Feld Jaeger bataillon Nr. 24* (k.u.k. Field Jaeger Battalion Nr. 24)

25. *k.u.k. Feld Jaeger bataillon Nr. 25* (k.u.k. Field Jaeger Battalion Nr. 25)

26. *k.u.k. Feld Jaeger bataillon Nr. 26* (k.u.k. Field Jaeger Battalion Nr. 26)

27. *k.u.k. Feld Jaeger bataillon Nr. 27* (k.u.k. Field Jaeger Battalion Nr. 27)

28. *k.u.k. Feld Jaeger bataillon Nr. 28* (k.u.k. Field Jaeger Battalion Nr. 28)

29. *k.u.k. Feld Jaeger bataillon Nr. 29* (k.u.k. Field Jaeger Battalion Nr. 29)

30. *k.u.k. Feld Jaeger bataillon Nr. 30* (k.u.k. Field Jaeger Battalion Nr. 30)

31. *k.u.k. Feld Jaeger bataillon Nr. 31 (*k.u.k. Field Jaeger Battalion Nr. 31)

32. *k.u.k. Feld Jaeger bataillon Nr. 32* (k.u.k. Field Jaeger Battalion Nr. 32)

Bosnia-Herzegovina Infantry Regiments

1. *k.u.k. Bosnisch-Hercegovinisches Infantrie Regiment Nr. 1* (k.u.k. Bosnia-Herzegovina Infantry Regiment No. 1)

2. *k.u.k. Bosnisch-Hercegovinisches Infantrie Regiment Nr. 2* (k.u.k. Bosnia-Herzegovina Infantry Regiment No. 2)

3. *k.u.k. Bosnisch-Hercegovinisches Infantrie Regiment Nr. 3* (k.u.k. Bosnia-Herzegovina Infantry Regiment No. 3)

4. *k.u.k. Bosnisch-Hercegovinisches Infantrie Regiment Nr. 4* (k.u.k. Bosnia-Herzegovina Infantry Regiment No. 4)

Dragoon Regiments

1. *k.u.k. Dragoner Regiment Kaiser Franz Nr. 1* (k.u.k. Dragoon Regiment

Kaiser Franz No. 1)

2. *k.u.k. Dragoner Regiment Graf Paar Nr. 2* (k.u.k. Dragoon Regiment Count Paar No. 2)

3. *k.u.k. Dragoner Regiment Friedrich August Koenig von Sachsen Nr. 3* (k.u.k. Dragoon Regiment Friedrich August King of Saxony No. 3)

4. *k.u.k. Dragoner Regiment Kaiser Ferdinand Nr. 4* (k.u.k. Dragoon Regiment Kaiser Ferdinand No. 4)

5. *k.u.k. Dragoner Regiment Nicholaus I. Kaiser von Russland Nr. 5* (k.u.k. Dragoon Regiment Nicholas I Emperor of Russia No. 5)

6. *k.u.k. Dragoner Regiment Friedrich Franz IV. Grossherzog von Mecklenburg- Schwerin Nr. 6* (k.u.k. Dragoon Regiment Friedrich Franz IV. Grand Duke of Mecklenburg- Schwerin No. 6)

7. *k.u.k. Dragoner Regiment Herzog von Lothringen Nr. 7* (k.u.k. Dragoon Regiment Duke of Lothringen No. 7)

8. *k.u.k. Dragoner Regiment Graf Montecuccoli Nr. 8* (k.u.k. Dragoon Regiment Count Montecuccoli No. 8)

9. *k.u.k. Dragoner Regiment Erzherzog Albrecht Nr. 9* (k.u.k. Dragoon Regiment Archduke Albrecht No. 9)

10. *k.u.k. Dragoner Regiment Fuerst von Liechtenstein Nr. 10* (k.u.k. Dragoon Regiment Prince of Liechtenstein No. 10)

11. *k.u.k. Dragoner Regiment Kaiser Nr. 11* (k.u.k. Dragoon Regiment Kaiser No. 11)

12. *k.u.k. Dragoner Regiment Nicholaus Nikolajewitsch Grossfuerst von Russland Nr. 12* (k.u.k. Dragoon Regiment Nicholas Nikolajewitsch Grand Duke of Russia No. 12)

13. *k.u.k. Dragoner Regiment Eugen Prinz von Savoyen Nr. 13* (k.u.k. Dragoon Regiment Eugene Prince of Savoy No. 13)

k.u.k. Dragoner Regiment (k.u.k. Dragoon Regiment

14. *k.u.k. Dragoner Regiment Fuerst zu Windisch Graetz Nr. 14* (k.u.k. Dragoon Regiment Prince to Windisch Graetz No. 14)

15. *k.u.k. Dragoner Regiment Erzherzog Joseph Nr. 15* (k.u.k. Dragoon Regiment Archduke Joseph No. 15)

Hussar Regiments

1. *k.u.k Husaren Regiment Kaiser Nr. 1* (k.u.k Hussar Regiment Kaiser No. 1)

2. *k.u.k Husaren Regiment Friedrich Leopold Prinz von Preussen Nr. 2* (k.u.k Hussar Regiment Friedrich Leopold Prince of Prussia No. 2)

3. *k.u.k Husaren Regiment Graf von Hadik Nr. 3* (k.u.k Hussar Regiment Count of Hadik No. 3)

4. *k.u.k. Husaren Regiment Herzog von Konnaught und Strathearn Nr. 4* (k.u.k Hussar Regiment Duke of Konnaught and Strathearn No. 4)

5. *k.u.k. Husaren Regiment Graf Radetzky Nr. 5* (k.u.k Hussar Regiment Count Radetzky No. 5)

6. *k.u.k. Husaren Regiment Wilhelm II. Koenig von Wuerttemberg Nr. 6* (k.u.k Hussar Regiment Wilhelm II. KIng of Würtemberg No. 6)

7. *k.u.k. Husaren Regiment Wilhelm II. Deutscher Kaiser und Koenig von Preussen Nr. 7* (k.u.k Hussar Regiment Wilhelm II. German Emperor and King of Prussia No. 7)

8. *k.u.k. Husaren Regiment von Tersztyásky Nr. 8* (k.u.k Hussar Regiment of Tersztyásky No. 8)

9. *k.u.k. Husaren Regiment Graf Nádasdy Nr. 9* (k.u.k Hussar Regiment Count Nádasdy No. 9)

10. *k.u.k. Husaren Regiment Friedrich Wilhelm III. Koenig von Preussen Nr. 10* (k.u.k Hussar Regiment Friedrich Wilhelm III. King of Prussia No. 10)

11. *k.u.k. Husaren Regiment Ferdinand I. Koenig der Bulgaren Nr. 11* (k.u.k Hussar Regiment Ferdinand I. King of the Bulgarians No. 11)

12. *k.u.k. Husaren Regiment Nr. 12* (k.u.k Hussar Regiment No. 12)

13. *k.u.k. Jazygier und Kumanier Husaren Regiment Wilhelm Kronprinz des Deutschen Reiches und Kronprinz von Preussen Nr. 13* (k.u.k. Jazygier and Kumanier Hussar Regiment Wilhelm Crown Prince of the German Reich and Crown Prince from Prussia No. 13)

14. *k.u.k. Husaren Regiment von Kolossvary Nr. 14* (k.u.k. Hussar Regiment of Kolossvary No. 14)

15. *k.u.k. Husaren Regiment Erzherzog Franz Salvator Nr. 15* (k.u.k. Hussar Regiment Archduke Franz Salvator No. 15)

16. *k.u.k. Husaren Regiment Graf Uxkull-Gyllenband Nr. 16* (k.u.k. Hussar Regiment Count Uxkull-Gyllenband No. 16)

Ulan Regiments

1. *k.u.k. Ulanen Regiment Ritter von Brudermann Nr. 1* (k.u.k. Ulan Regiment Knight of Brudermann No. 1)

2. *k.u.k. Ulanen Regiment Furst zu Schwarzenberg Nr. 2* (k.u.k. Ulan Regiment Prince to Schwarzenberg No. 2)

3. *k.u.k. Ulanen Regiment Erzherzog Karl Nr. 3* (k.u.k. Ulan Regiment Archduke Charles No. 3)

4. *k.u.k. Ulanen Regiment Kaiser Nr. 4* (k.u.k. Ulan Regiment Kaiser (Emperor) No. 4)

5. *k.u.k. Ulanen Regiment Nikolaus II. Kaiser von Russland Nr. 5* (k.u.k. Ulan Regiment Nicholas II Emperor (Czar) of Russia No. 5)

6. *k.u.k. Ulanen Regiment Kaiser Joseph II. Nr. 6* (k.u.k. Ulan Regiment Emperor Joseph II No. 6)

7. *k.u.k. Ulanen Regiment Erzherzog Franz Ferdinand Nr. 7* (k.u.k. Ulan Regiment Archduke Franz Ferdinand No. 7)

8. *k.u.k. Ulanen Regiment Graf Auersperg Nr. 8* (k.u.k. Ulan Regiment Count Auersperg No. 8)

9. Regiment 9 was turned into Dragoon and Hussar Regiment

10. Regiment 10 was turned into Dragoon and Hussar Regiment

11. *k.u.k. Ulanen Regiment Alexander II Kaiser von Russland Nr.* 11(k.u.k. Ulan Regiment Alexander II Kaiser (Czar)of Russia No. 11)

12. *k.u.k. Ulanen Regiment Graf Huyn Nr. 12* (k.u.k. Ulan Regiment Count Huyn No. 12)

13. *k.u.k. Ulanen Regiment von Bohm-Ermolli Nr. 13* (k.u.k. Ulan Regiment of Bohm-Ermolli No. 13)

Field Cannon Regiments

1. *k.u.k. Feldkanonen Regiment Nr. 1* (k.u.k. Field Cannon Regiment No. 1)

2. *k.u.k. Feldkanonen Regiment Nr. 2* (k.u.k. Field Cannon Regiment No. 2)

3. *k.u.k. Feldkanonen Regiment* Nr. 3 (k.u.k. Field Cannon Regiment No. 3)

4. *k.u.k. Feldkanonen Regiment Nr. 4* (k.u.k. Field Cannon Regiment No. 4)

5. *k.u.k. Feldkanonen Regiment Nr. 5* (k.u.k. Field Cannon Regiment No. 5)

6. *k.u.k. Feldkanonen Regiment Nr. 6* (k.u.k. Field Cannon Regiment No. 6)

7. *k.u.k. Feldkanonen Regiment Nr. 7* (k.u.k. Field Cannon Regiment No. 7)

8. *k.u.k. Feldkanonen Regiment Nr. 8* (k.u.k. Field Cannon Regiment No. 8)

9. *k.u.k. Feldkanonen Regiment Nr. 9* (k.u.k. Field Cannon Regiment No. 9)

10. *k.u.k. Feldkanonen Regiment Nr. 10* (k.u.k. Field Cannon Regiment No. 10)

11. *k.u.k. Feldkanonen Regiment Nr. 11* (k.u.k. Field Cannon Regiment No. 11)

12. *k.u.k. Feldkanonen Regiment Nr. 12* (k.u.k. Field Cannon Regiment No. 12)

13. *k.u.k. Feldkanonen Regiment Nr. 13* (k.u.k. Field Cannon Regiment No. 13)

14. *k.u.k. Feldkanonen Regiment Nr. 14* (k.u.k. Field Cannon Regiment No. 14)

15. *k.u.k. Feldkanonen Regiment Nr. 15* (k.u.k. Field Cannon Regiment No. 15)

16. *k.u.k. Feldkanonen Regiment Nr. 16* (k.u.k. Field Cannon Regiment No. 16)

17. *k.u.k. Feldkanonen Regiment Nr. 17* (k.u.k. Field Cannon Regiment No. 17)

18. *k.u.k. Feldkanonen Regiment Nr. 18* (k.u.k. Field Cannon Regiment No. 18)

19. *k.u.k. Feldkanonen Regiment Nr. 19* (k.u.k. Field Cannon Regiment No. 19)

20. *k.u.k. Feldkanonen Regiment Nr. 20* (k.u.k. Field Cannon Regiment No. 20)

21. *k.u.k. Feldkanonen Regiment Nr. 21* (k.u.k. Field Cannon Regiment No. 21)

22. *k.u.k. Feldkanonen Regiment Nr. 22* (k.u.k. Field Cannon Regiment No. 22)

23. *k.u.k. Feldkanonen Regiment Nr. 23* (k.u.k. Field Cannon Regiment No. 23)

24. *k.u.k. Feldkanonen Regiment Nr. 24* (k.u.k. Field Cannon Regiment No. 24)

25. *k.u.k. Feldkanonen Regiment Nr. 25* (k.u.k. Field Cannon Regiment No. 25)

26. *k.u.k. Feldkanonen Regiment Nr. 26* (k.u.k. Field Cannon Regiment No. 26)

27. *k.u.k. Feldkanonen Regiment Nr. 1* (k.u.k. Field Cannon Regiment No. 27)

28. *k.u.k. Feldkanonen Regiment Nr. 28* (k.u.k. Field Cannon Regiment No. 28)

29. *k.u.k. Feldkanonen Regiment Nr. 29* (k.u.k. Field Cannon Regiment No. 29)

30. *k.u.k. Feldkanonen Regiment Nr. 30* (k.u.k. Field Cannon Regiment No. 30)

31. *k.u.k. Feldkanonen Regiment Nr. 31* (k.u.k. Field Cannon Regiment No. 31)

32. *k.u.k. Feldkanonen Regiment Nr. 32* (k.u.k. Field Cannon Regiment No. 32)

33. *k.u.k. Feldkanonen Regiment Nr. 33* (k.u.k. Field Cannon Regiment No. 33)

34. *k.u.k. Feldkanonen Regiment Nr. 34* (k.u.k. Field Cannon Regiment No. 34)

35. *k.u.k. Feldkanonen Regiment Nr. 35* (k.u.k. Field Cannon Regiment No. 35)

36. *k.u.k. Feldkanonen Regiment Nr. 36* (k.u.k. Field Cannon Regiment No. 36)

37. *k.u.k. Feldkanonen Regiment Nr. 37* (k.u.k. Field Cannon Regiment No. 37)

38. *k.u.k. Feldkanonen Regiment Nr. 38* (k.u.k. Field Cannon Regiment No. 38)

39. *k.u.k. Feldkanonen Regiment Nr. 39* (k.u.k. Field Cannon Regiment No. 39)

40. *k.u.k. Feldkanonen Regiment Nr. 40* (k.u.k. Field Cannon Regiment No. 40)

41. *k.u.k. Feldkanonen Regiment Nr. 41* (k.u.k. Field Cannon Regiment No. 41)

42. *k.u.k. Feldkanonen Regiment Nr. 42* (k.u.k. Field Cannon Regiment No. 42)

Field Howitzer Regiments

1. *k.u.k. Feldhaubitz Regiment Sergius Mihailowitsch Grossfurst von Russland Nr. 1* (k.u.k. Field Howitzer Regiment Sergius Mihailowitsch Grand Duke of Russia No. 1)

2. *k.u.k. Feldhaubitz Regiment Graf von Geldern-Egmond Nr. 2* (k.u.k. Field Howitzer Regiment Count of Geldern-Egmond No. 2)

3. *k.u.k. Feldhaubitz Regiment Erzherzog Wilhelm Nr. 3* (k.u.k. Field Howitzer Regiment Archduke Wilhelm No. 3)

4. *k.u.k. Feldhaubitz Regiment Nr. 4*(k.u.k. Field Howitzer Regiment No. 4)

5. *k.u.k. Feldhaubitz Regiment Erzherzog Albrecht Nr. 5* (k.u.k. Field Howitzer Regiment Archduke Albrecht No. 5)

6. *k.u.k. Feldhaubitz Regiment Erzherzog Franz Ferdinand Nr. 6*(k.u.k. Field Howitzer Regiment Archduke Franz Ferdinand No. 6)

7. *k.u.k. Feldhaubitz Regiment Leopold Prinz von Bayern Nr. 7*(k.u.k. Field Howitzer Regiment Leopold Prince of Bayern No. 7)

8. *k.u.k. Feldhaubitz Regiment Kaiser Nr. 8* (k.u.k. Field Howitzer Regiment Emperor No. 8)

9. *k.u.k. Feldhaubitz Regiment Joseph Wendel Fuerst von Liechtenstein Nr. 9* (k.u.k. Field Howitzer Regiment Joseph Wendel Prince of Liechtenstein No. 9)

10. *k.u.k. Feldhaubitz Regiment Nr. 10* (k.u.k. Field Howitzer Regiment No. 10)

11. *k.u.k. Feldhaubitz Regiment Freiherr von Smola Nr. 11* (k.u.k. Field Howitzer Regiment Baron of Smola No. 11)

12. *k.u.k. Feldhaubitz Regiment Georg V. Koenig von Grossbritannien und Irland, Kaiser von Indien Nr. 11* (k.u.k. Field Howitzer Regiment George V. King of Great Britain and Ireland, Emperor of India Nr. 11)

13. *k.u.k. Feldhaubitz Regiment Erzherzog Leopold Salvator Nr. 13* (k.u.k. Field Howitzer Regiment Archduke Leopold Salvator No. 13)

14. *k.u.k. Feldhaubitz Regiment Ritter von Krobatin Nr. 14* (k.u.k. Field Howitzer Regiment Knight of Krobatin No. 14)

Heavy Field Howitzer Divisions

1. *k.u.k. Schwere Haubitz Division Nr. 1* (k.u.k. Heavy Field Howitzer division Nr. 1)

2 *k.u.k. Schwere Haubitz Division Nr. 2* (k.u.k. Heavy Field Howitzer division Nr. 2)

3. *k.u.k. Schwere Haubitz Division Nr. 3* (k.u.k. Heavy Field Howitzer division Nr. 3)

4. *k.u.k. Schwere Haubitz Division Nr. 4* (k.u.k. Heavy Field Howitzer division Nr. 4)

5. *k.u.k. Schwere Haubitz Division Nr. 5* (k.u.k. Heavy Field Howitzer division Nr. 5)

6. *k.u.k. Schwere Haubitz Division Nr. 6* (k.u.k. Heavy Field Howitzer division Nr. 6)

7. *k.u.k. Schwere Haubitz Division Nr. 7* (k.u.k. Heavy Field Howitzer division Nr. 7)

8. *k.u.k. Schwere Haubitz Division Nr. 8* (k.u.k. Heavy Field Howitzer division Nr. 8)

9. *k.u.k. Schwere Haubitz Division Nr. 9* (k.u.k. Heavy Field Howitzer division Nr. 9)

10. *k.u.k. Schwere Haubitz Division Nr. 10* (k.u.k. Heavy Field Howitzer division Nr. 10)

11. *k.u.k. Schwere Haubitz Division Nr. 11* (k.u.k. Heavy Field Howitzer division Nr. 11)

12. *k.u.k. Schwere Haubitz Division Nr. 12* (k.u.k. Heavy Field Howitzer division Nr. 12)

13. *k.u.k. Schwere Haubitz Division Nr. 13* (k.u.k. Heavy Field Howitzer division Nr. 13)

14. *k.u.k. Schwere Haubitz Division Nr. 14* (k.u.k. Heavy Field Howitzer division Nr. 14)

Mounted/Horse Artillery Divisions

1. *k.u.k. Reitende Artillerie Division Nr. 1* (k.u.k. Mounted/Horse Artillery Division No. 1)

2. *k.u.k. Reitende Artillerie Division Nr. 2* (k.u.k. Mounted/Horse Artillery Division No. 2)

3. *k.u.k. Reitende Artillerie Division Nr. 3* (k.u.k. Mounted/Horse Artillery Division No. 3)

4. *k.u.k. Reitende Artillerie Division Nr. 4* (k.u.k. Mounted/Horse Artillery Division No. 4)

5. *k.u.k. Reitende Artillerie Division Nr. 5* (k.u.k. Mounted/Horse Artillery Division No. 5)

6. *k.u.k. Reitende Artillerie Division Nr. 6* (k.u.k. Mounted/Horse Artillery Division No. 6)

7. *k.u.k. Reitende Artillerie Division Nr. 7* (k.u.k. Mounted/Horse Artillery Division No. 7)

8. *k.u.k. Reitende Artillerie Division Nr. 8* (k.u.k. Mounted/Horse Artillery Division No. 8)

9. *k.u.k. Reitende Artillerie Division Nr. 9* (k.u.k. Mounted/Horse Artillery Division No. 9)

10. *k.u.k. Reitende Artillerie Division Nr. 10* (k.u.k. Mounted/Horse Artillery Division No. 10)

11. *k.u.k. Reitende Artillerie Division Nr. 11* (k.u.k. Mounted/Horse Artillery Division No. 11)

Mountain Artillery Regiments

1. *k.u.k. Gebirgsartillerie Regiment Nr. 1* (k.u.k. Mountain Artillery Regiment No. 1)

2. *k.u.k. Gebirgsartillerie Regiment Nr. 2* (k.u.k. Mountain Artillery Regiment No. 2)

3. *k.u.k. Gebirgsartillerie Regiment Nr. 3* (k.u.k. Mountain Artillery Regiment No. 3)

4. *k.u.k. Gebirgsartillerie Regiment Nr. 4* (k.u.k. Mountain Artillery Regiment No. 4)

5. *k.u.k. Gebirgsartillerie Regiment Nr. 5* (k.u.k. Mountain Artillery Regiment No. 5)

6. *k.u.k. Gebirgsartillerie Regiment Nr. 6* (k.u.k. Mountain Artillery Regiment No. 6)

7. *k.u.k. Gebirgsartillerie Regiment Nr. 7* (k.u.k. Mountain Artillery Regiment No. 7)

8. *k.u.k. Gebirgsartillerie Regiment Nr. 8* (k.u.k. Mountain Artillery regiment No. 8)

9. *k.u.k. Gebirgsartillerie Regiment Nr. 9* (k.u.k. Mountain Artillery Regiment No. 9)

10. *k.u.k. Gebirgsartillerie Regiment Nr. 10* (k.u.k. Mountain Artillery Regiment No. 10)

11. *k.u.k. Gebirgsartillerie Regiment Nr. 11* (k.u.k. Mountain Artillery Regiment No. 11)

12. *k.u.k. Gebirgsartillerie Regiment Nr. 12* (k.u.k. Mountain Artillery Regiment No. 12)

13. *k.u.k. Gebirgsartillerie Regiment Nr. 13* (k.u.k. Mountain Artillery Regiment No. 13)

14. *k.u.k. Gebirgsartillerie Regiment Nr. 14* (k.u.k. Mountain Artillery Regiment No. 14)

Fortress Artillery Regiments

1. *k.u.k Festungs Artillerie Regiment Kaiser Nr. 1* (k.u.k Fortress Artillery Regiment Kaiser No. 1)

2. *k.u.k Festungs Artillerie Regiment Freiherr von Beschi Nr. 2* (k.u.k Fortress Artillery Regiment Baron of Beschi No. 2)

3. *k.u.k Festungs Artillerie Regiment Fürst Kinsky Nr. 3* (k.u.k Fortress Artillery Regiment Prince Kinsky No. 3)

4. *k.u.k Festungs Artillerie Regiment Graf Colloredo-Mels Nr. 4* (k.u.k Fortress Artillery Regiment Count Colloredo-Mels No. 4)

5. *k.u.k Festungs Artillerie Regiment Freiherr von Rouvroy Nr. 5* (k.u.k Fortress Artillery Regiment Baron of Rouvoy No. 5)

6. *k.u.k Festungs Artillerie Regiment von Kollarz Nr. 6* (k.u.k Fortress Artillery Regiment of Kollarz No.6)

Fortress Artillery Battalions

1. *k.u.k. Festungs Artillerie Bataillon Nr. 1* (k.u.k. Fortress Artillery Battalion No. 1)

2. *k.u.k. Festungs Artillerie Bataillon Nr. 2* (k.u.k. Fortress Artillery Battalion No. 2)

3. *k.u.k. Festungs Artillerie Bataillon Nr. 3* (k.u.k. Fortress Artillery Battalion No. 3)

4. *k.u.k. Festungs Artillerie Bataillon Nr. 4* (k.u.k. Fortress Artillery Battalion No. 4)

5. *k.u.k. Festungs Artillerie Bataillon Nr. 5* (k.u.k. Fortress Artillery Battalion No. 5)

6. *k.u.k. Festungs Artillerie Bataillon Nr. 6* (k.u.k. Fortress Artillery Battalion No. 6)

7. *k.u.k. Festungs Artillerie Bataillon Nr. 7* (k.u.k. Fortress Artillery Battalion No. 7)

8. *k.u.k. Festungs Artillerie Bataillon Nr. 8* (k.u.k. Fortress Artillery Battalion No. 8)

Pioneer (Sapper) Battalions

1. *k.u.k. Sappeur Bataillon Nr. 1* (k.u.k. Sapper Battalion No. 1)
2. *k.u.k. Sappeur Bataillon Nr. 2* (k.u.k. Sapper Battalion No. 2)
3. *k.u.k. Sappeur Bataillon Nr. 3* (k.u.k. Sapper Battalion No. 3)
4. *k.u.k. Sappeur Bataillon Nr. 4* (k.u.k. Sapper Battalion No. 4)
5. *k.u.k. Sappeur Bataillon Nr. 5* (k.u.k. Sapper Battalion No. 5)
6. *k.u.k. Sappeur Bataillon Nr. 6* (k.u.k. Sapper Battalion No. 6)
7. *k.u.k. Sappeur Bataillon Nr. 7* (k.u.k. Sapper Battalion No. 7)
8. *k.u.k. Sappeur Bataillon Nr. 8* (k.u.k. Sapper Battalion No. 8)
9. *k.u.k. Sappeur Bataillon Nr. 9* (k.u.k. Sapper Battalion No. 9)
10. *k.u.k. Sappeur Bataillon Nr. 10* (k.u.k. Sapper Battalion No. 10)
11. *k.u.k. Sappeur Bataillon Nr. 11* (k.u.k. Sapper Battalion No. 11)
12. *k.u.k. Sappeur Bataillon Nr. 12* (k.u.k. Sapper Battalion No. 12)
13. *k.u.k. Sappeur Bataillon Nr. 13* (k.u.k. Sapper Battalion No. 13)
14. *k.u.k. Sappeur Bataillon Nr. 14* (k.u.k. Sapper Battalion No. 14)

Pioneer Battalions

1. *k.u.k. Pionier Bataillon Nr. 1* (k.u.k. Pioneer Battalion No. 1)
2. *k.u.k. Pionier Bataillon Nr. 2* (k.u.k. Pioneer Battalion No. 2)
3. *k.u.k. Pionier Bataillon Nr. 3* (k.u.k. Pioneer Battalion No. 3)
4. *k.u.k. Pionier Bataillon Nr. 4* (k.u.k. Pioneer Battalion No. 4)
5. *k.u.k. Pionier Bataillon Nr. 5* (k.u.k. Pioneer Battalion No. 5)
6. *k.u.k. Pionier Bataillon Nr. 6* (k.u.k. Pioneer Battalion No. 6)

7. *k.u.k. Pionier Bataillon Nr. 7* (k.u.k. Pioneer Battalion No. 7)
8. *k.u.k. Pionier Bataillon Nr. 8* (k.u.k. Pioneer Battalion No. 8)
9. *k.u.k. Pionier Bataillon Nr. 9* (k.u.k. Pioneer Battalion No. 9)
10. *k.u.k. Pionier Bataillon Nr. 10* (k.u.k. Pioneer Battalion No. 10)

Landwehr (Reserve) Infantry Regiments

1. *k.u.k. Landwehr Infanterie Regiment Wien Nr. 1* (k.u.k. Reserve Infantry Regiment Vienna No. 1)
2. *k.u.k. Landwehr Infanterie Regiment Linz Nr. 2* (k.u.k. Reserve Infantry Regiment Linz No. 2)
3. *k.u.k. Landwehr Infanterie Regiment Graz Nr. 3* (k.u.k. Reserve Infantry Regiment Graz No. 3)
4. *k.u.k. Landwehr Infanterie Regiment Klagenfurt Nr. 4* (k.u.k. Reserve Infantry Regiment Klagenfurt No. 4)
5. *k.u.k. Landwehr Infanterie Regiment Pola Nr. 5* (k.u.k. Reserve Infantry Regiment Pola No. 5)
6. *k.u.k. Landwehr Infanterie Regiment Eger Nr. 6* (k.u.k. Reserve Infantry Regiment Eger No. 6)
7. *k.u.k. Landwehr Infanterie Regiment Pilsen Nr.7* (k.u.k. Reserve Infantry Regiment Pilsen No. 7)
8. *k.u.k. Landwehr Infanterie Regiment Prag Nr. 8* (k.u.k. Reserve Infantry Regiment Prague No. 8)
9. *k.u.k. Landwehr Infanterie Regiment Leitmeritz Nr. 9* (k.u.k. Reserve Infantry Regiment Leitmeritz No. 9)
10. *k.u.k. Landwehr Infanterie Regiment Jungbunzlau Nr. 10* (k.u.k. Reserve Infantry Regiment Jungbunzlau No. 10)
11. *k.u.k. Landwehr Infanterie Regiment Jicin Nr. 11* (k.u.k. Reserve Infantry Regiment Jicin No. 11)
12. *k.u.k. Landwehr Infanterie Regiment Caslau Nr. 12* (k.u.k. Reserve Infantry Regiment Caslau No. 12)
13. *k.u.k. Landwehr Infanterie Regiment Olmuetz Nr. 13* (k.u.k. Reserve Infantry Regiment Olmuetz No. 13)
14. *k.u.k. Landwehr Infanterie Regiment Bruenn Nr. 14* (k.u.k. Reserve Infantry Regiment Bruenn No. 14)
15. *k.u.k. Landwehr Infanterie Regiment Troppau Nr. 15* (k.u.k. Reserve Infantry Troppau Regiment No. 15)
16. *k.u.k. Landwehr Infanterie Regiment Krakau Nr. 16* (k.u.k. Reserve Infantry Regiment Krakow No. 16)
17. *k.u.k. Landwehr Infanterie Regiment Rzeszow Nr. 17* (k.u.k. Reserve Infantry Regiment Rzeszow No. 17)
18. *k.u.k. Landwehr Infanterie Regiment Przemysl Nr. 18*(k.u.k. Reserve Infantry Regiment Przemysl No. 18)
19. *k.u.k. Landwehr Infanterie Regiment Lemberg Nr. 19* (k.u.k. Reserve Infantry Regiment Lemberg No. 19)
20. *k.u.k. Landwehr Infanterie Regiment Stanislau Nr. 20* (k.u.k. Reserve Infantry Regiment Stanislau No. 20)
21. *k.u.k. Landwehr Infanterie St. Poelten Regiment Nr. 21*(k.u.k. Reserve Infantry Regiment St. Poelten No. 21)
22. *k.u.k. Landwehr Infanterie Regiment Czernowitz Nr. 22* (k.u.k. Reserve Infantry Regiment Czernowitz No. 22)
23. *k.u.k. Landwehr Infanterie Regiment Sebenico Nr. 23* (k.u.k. Reserve Infantry Regiment Sebernico No. 23)
24. *k.u.k. Landwehr Infanterie Regiment Wien Nr. 24* (k.u.k. Reserve Infantry Regiment Vienna No. 24)
25. *k.u.k. Landwehr Infanterie Regiment Kremsier Nr.* 25 (k.u.k. Reserve Infantry Regiment Kremsier No. 25)
26. *k.u.k. Landwehr Infanterie Regiment Marburg Nr. 26* (k.u.k. Reserve Infantry Regiment Marburg No. 26)
27. *k.u.k. Landwehr Infanterie Regiment Laibach Nr. 27* (k.u.k. Reserve Infantry Regiment Laibach No. 27)
28. *k.u.k. Landwehr Infanterie Regiment Pisek Nr. 28* (k.u.k. Reserve Infantry Regiment Pisek No. 28)
29. *k.u.k. Landwehr Infanterie Regiment Budweis Nr. 29* (k.u.k. Reserve Infantry Regiment Budweis No. 29)
30. *k.u.k. Landwehr Infanterie Regiment Hohenmauth Nr. 30* (k.u.k. Reserve Infantry Regiment Hohenmauth No. 30)
31. *k.u.k. Landwehr Infanterie Regiment Teschen Nr. 31* (k.u.k. Reserve Infantry Regiment Teschen No. 31)
32. *k.u.k. Landwehr Infanterie Regiment Neusandez Nr. 32* (k.u.k. Reserve Infantry Regiment Neusandez No. 32)
33. *k.u.k. Landwehr Infanterie Regiment Stryi Nr. 33* (k.u.k. Reserve Infantry Regiment Stryi No. 33)
34. *k.u.k. Landwehr Infanterie Regiment Jaroslau Nr. 34* (k.u.k. Reserve Infantry Regiment Jaroslau No. 34)
35. *k.u.k. Landwehr Infanterie Regiment Zloczow Nr. 35* (k.u.k. Reserve Infantry Regiment Zloczow No. 35)
36. *k.u.k. Landwehr Infanterie Regiment Kolomea Nr. 36* (k.u.k. Reserve Infantry Regiment Kolomea No. 36)
37. *k.u.k. Landwehr Infanterie Regiment Gravosa Nr. 37* (k.u.k. Reserve Infantry Regiment Gravosa No. 37)

Landwehr Cavalry

1. *k.u.k. Landwehr Ulanen Regiment Nr. 1*(k.u.k. Ulan Reserve Regiment No.1)
2. *k.u.k. Landwehr Ulanen Regiment Nr. 2* (k.u.k. Ulan Reserve Regiment No. 2)
3. *k.u.k. Landwehr Ulanen Regiment Nr. 3* (k.u.k. Ulan Reserve Regiment No. 3)
4. *k.u.k. Landwehr Ulanen Regiment Nr. 4* (k.u.k. Ulan Reserve Regiment No. 4)
5. *k.u.k. Landwehr Ulanen Regiment Nr. 5* (k.u.k. Ulan Reserve Regiment No. 5)
6. *k.u.k. Landwehr Ulanen Regiment Nr. 6* (k.u.k. Ulan Reserve Regiment No. 6)

Landwehr Field Cannon/Howitzer Divisions

1. k.u.k. Landwehr Feldkanonen Division Nr. 13 (k.u.k. Reserve Field Cannon Division No. 13)
2. *k.u.k. Landwehr Feldkanonen Division Nr. 21* (k.u.k. Reserve Field Cannon Division No. 21)
3. *k.u.k. Landwehr Feldkanonen Division Nr. 22* (k.u.k. Reserve Field Cannon Division No. 22)
4. *k.u.k. Landwehr Feldkanonen Division Nr. 26* (k.u.k. Reserve Field Cannon Division No. 26)
5. *k.u.k. Landwehr Feldkanonen Division Nr. 43* (k.u.k. Reserve Field Cannon Division No. 43)
6. *k.u.k. Landwehr Feldkanonen Division Nr. 44* (k.u.k. Reserve Field Cannon Division No. 44)
7. *k.u.k. Landwehr Feldkanonen Division Nr. 45* (k.u.k. Reserve Field Cannon Division No. 45)
8. *k.u.k. Landwehr Feldkanonen Division Nr. 46* (k.u.k. Reserve Field Cannon Division No. 46)
9. *k.u.k Landwehr Feldhaubitz Division Nr. 13* (k.u.k Reserve Feld Howitzer Division No. 13)
10. *k.u.k Landwehr Feldhaubitz Division Nr. 21* (k.u.k Reserve Feld Howitzer Division No. 21)
11. *k.u.k Landwehr Feldhaubitz Division Nr. 22* (k.u.k Reserve Feld Howitzer Division No. 22)
12. *k.u.k Landwehr Feldhaubitz Division Nr. 26* (k.u.k Reserve Feld Howitzer Division No. 26)

13. *k.u.k Landwehr Feldhaubitz Division Nr. 43* (k.u.k Reserve Feld Howitzer Division No. 43)

14. *k.u.k Landwehr Feldhaubitz Division Nr. 44* (k.u.k Reserve Feld Howitzer Division No. 44)

15. *k.u.k Landwehr Feldhaubitz Division Nr. 45* (k.u.k Reserve Feld Howitzer Division No. 45)

16. *k.u.k Landwehr Feldhaubitz Division Nr. 46* (k.u.k Reserve Feld Howitzer Division No. 46)

Hungarian Infantry Regiments

1. *m.k. Budapesti 1 honved gyalog ezred* (k.u.k. Hungarian Infantry Regiment 1 Budapest)

2. *m.k. Gyuali 2. honved gyalog ezred* (k.u.k. Hungarian Infantry Regiment Gyulai No. 2)

3. *m.k. Debreczeni 3. honved gyalog ezred* (k.u.k. Hungarian Infantry Regiment Debreczen No. 3)

4. *m.k Nagyváradi 4. honved gyalog ezred* (k.u.k. Hungarian Infantry Regiment Nagyvárad No. 4)

5. *m.k. Szegedi 5. honved gyalog ezred* (k.u.k. Hungarian Infantry Regiment Szeged No.5)

6. *m.k. Szabadkai 6. honved gyalog ezred* (k.u.k. Hungarian Infantry Regiment Szabadka No. 6)

7. *m.k. Verseci 7. honved gyalog ezred* (k.u.k. Hungarian Infantry Regiment Versecz No. 7)

8. *m.k. Lugosi 8. honved gyalog ezred* (k.u.k. Hungarian Infantry Regiment Lugos No. 8)

9. *m.k. Kassai 9. honved gyalog ezred* (k.u.k. Hungarian Infantry Regiment Kassa No. 9)

10. *m.k. Miskolci 10. honved gyalog ezred* (k.u.k. Hungarian Infantry Regiment Mislolcz No. 10)

11. *m.k. Munkácsi 11. honved gyalog ezred* (k.u.k. Hungarian Infantry Regiment Munkács No. 11)

12. *m.k. Szatmári-Nemeti 12. honved gyalog ezred* (k.u.k. Hungarian Infantry Regiment Szatmár- Nemet)

13. *m.k. Pozonyi 13. honved gyalog ezred* (k.u.k. Hungarian Infantry Regiment Pozony No. 13)

14. *m.k. Nyitra 14. honved gyalog ezred* (k.u.k. Hungarian Infantry Regiment Nyitra No. 14)

15. *m.k. Trencseni 15. honved gyalog ezred* (k.u.k. Hungarian Infantry Regiment Trencsen No. 15)

16. *m.k. Beszterczebanyai 16. honved gyalog ezred* (k.u.k. Hungarian Infantry Regiment Beszterczebanya No. 16)

17. *m.k. Szekesfehervari 17. honved gyalog ezred* (k.u.k. Hungarian Infantry Regiment Szekesfehervar No. 17)

18. *m.k. Soproni 18. honved gyalog ezred* (k.u.k. Hungarian Infantry Regiment Sopron)

19. *m.k. Pecsi 19. honved gyalog ezred* (k.u.k. Hungarian Infantry Regiment Pecsi No. 19)

20. *m.k. Nagykanizsai 20. honved gyalog ezred* (k.u.k. Hungarian Infantry Regiment Nagykanizsa No. 20)

21. *m.k. Kolozsvári 21. honved gyalog ezred* (k.u.k. Hungarian Infantry Regiment Kolozsvár No. 21)

22. *m.k. Marosvasarhelyi 22. honved gyalog ezred* (k.u.k. Hungarian Infantry Regiment Marosvasarhely No. 22)

23. *m.k. Nagyszebeni 23. honved gyalog ezred* (k.u.k. Hungarian Infantry Regiment Nagyszeben No. 23)

24. *m.k. Brassoi 24. honved gyalog ezred* (k.u.k. Hungarian Infantry Regiment Brasso No. 24)

25. *m.k. Agrami 25. honved gyalog ezred* (k.u.k. Hungarian Infantry Regiment Agram No. 25)

26. *m.k. Karolyvarosi 26. honved gyalog ezred* (k.u.k. Hungarian Infantry Regiment Karolyvaros No. 26)

27. *m.k. Sziszeki 27. honved gyalog ezred* (k.u.k. Hungarian Infantry Regiment Szizek No. 27)

28. *m.k. Eszeki 28. honved gyalog ezred* (k.u.k. Hungarian Infantry Regiment Eszek No. 28)

29. *m.k. Budapesti 29. honved gyalog ezred* (k.u.k. Hungarian Infantry Regiment Budapest No. 29)

30. *m.k. Budapesti 30. honved gyalog ezred* (k.u.k. Hungarian Infantry Regiment Budapest No. 30)

31. *m.k. Veszpremi 31. honved gyalog ezred* (k.u.k. Hungarian Infantry Regiment Veszprem No. 30)

32. *m.k. Desi 32. honved gyalog ezred* (k.u.k. Hungarian Infantry Regiment Des No. 32)

Hungarian Hussar Regiments

1. *m.k. Budapesti 1. honved huszár ezred* (k.u.k. Hungarian Hussar Regiment Budapest No. 1)

2. *m.k. Debreczeni 2. honved huszár ezred* (k.u.k. Hungarian Hussar Regiment DebreczenNo. 2)

3. *m.k. Szegedi 3. honved huszár ezred* (k.u.k. Hungarian Hussar Regiment Szeged No. 3)

4. *m.k. Szabadkai 4. honved huszár ezred* (k.u.k. Hungarian Hussar Regiment Szabadka No. 4)

5. *m.k. Kassai 5. honved huszár ezred* (k.u.k. Hungarian Hussar Regiment Kassa No. 5)

6. *m.k. Zalaegerszegi 6. honved huszár ezred* (k.u.k. Hungarian Hussar Regiment Zalaegerszeg No. 6)

7. *m.k. Papai 7. honved huszár ezred* (k.u.k. Hungarian Hussar Regiment Papa No. 7)

8. *m.k. Pecsi 8. honved huszár ezred* (k.u.k. Hungarian Hussar Regiment Pecs No. 8)

9. *m.k. Marosvasarhelyi 9. honved huszár ezred* (k.u.k. Hungarian Hussar Regiment Marosvasarhely No. 9)

10. *m.k. Varasdi 10. honved huszár ezred* (k.u.k. Hungarian Hussar Regiment Warasdin No. 10)

Hungarian Artillery Regiments and Divisions

1. *m.k. 1 honved tábori agyus ezred* (k.u.k Hungarian Field Cannon Regiment No. 1)

8. *m.k. 8 honved tábori agyus ezred* (k.u.k Hungarian Field Cannon Regiment No. 8)

1. *m.k. 1. honved tábori agyus osztaly* (k.u.k Hungarian Field Cannon Division No. 1)

2. *m.k. 2. honved tábori agyus osztaly* (k.u.k Hungarian Field Cannon Division No. 2)

3. *m.k. 3. honved tábori agyus osztaly* (k.u.k Hungarian Field Cannon Division No. 3)

4. *m.k. 4. honved tábori agyus osztaly* (k.u.k Hungarian Field Cannon Division No. 4)

5. *m.k. 5. honved tábori agyus osztaly* (k.u.k Hungarian Field Cannon Division No. 5)

6. *m.k. 6. honved tábori agyus osztaly* (k.u.k Hungarian Field Cannon Division No. 6)

7. *m.k. 7. honved tábori agyus osztaly* (k.u.k Hungarian Field Cannon Division No. 7)

8. *m.k. 8. honved tábori agyus osztaly* (k.u.k Hungarian Field Cannon Division No. 8)

Further Reading

Le Armi e gli Equipaggiamenti dell'esercito Austria-Ungarn dal 1914 al 1918. Uniformi-Distintivi-Buffetterie. volume primo., Siro Offelli, Gino Rossato Editore. Via bella Venezia 2001.

230 pages. This book contains color photographs of Uniforms and Equipment of the Austro-Hungarian Army as well as black and white period photographs. Italian and German text.

Armi ed Equipaggiamenti dell'esercito Italiano nella Grande Guerra 1915-1918. Nevio Mantoan. Gino Rossato Editore. Via Bella Venezia 1996.

189 pages. This book contains black and white photos of WWI Italian army equipment, small artillery and machineguns and a color section on WWI Italian uniforms. Italian text.

L'Artiglieria Austro-Ungarica nella Grande Guerra. Filippo Cappelano. Gino Rossato Editore. Via Bella Venezia 2001.

242 pages. Black and white photos of artillery and crewmen as well as charts. Italian and German text.

Der Krieg der Grossväter 1914-1918. Die Vergessenen einer grossen Armee. Hans Magenschab. Verlag der Oesterreichen Staatsdruckerei,Wien 1993.

224 pages. Black and white period photos. German text.

Királyért és Hazáért Barcy Zoltán, Somogyi Gyõzõ Corvina. Hungary 1990.

244 pages. Color drawings. Hungarian text with German glossary.